Moon & Weather Lore

KEN RING

Copyright © 2002 Ken Ring
Second Edition 2014
All rights reserved.
ISBN: 978-0-86467-005-2

No part of this book may be reproduced or transmitted in any form or by any means, electronic or mechanical, including photocopying, recording, or any information storage and retrieval system without prior written permission of the author.

The moral right of the author to the copyright of this work as regards concept and expression of the manuscript has been asserted. Reproduction of any part only by written consent of the author.

In fond memory of Harry

TABLE OF CONTENTS

Introduction 1
Changes 11
Mythology 21
Cycles 31
Winds 35
When Rain Or Snow 63
Phases and Horns 71
Eclipses 83
Clouds 87
Mist, Frost & Fog 105
Earthquakes 109
Thunder, Lightning, Hail & Cyclones 113
Tornadoes, Cloudbursts & Waterspouts 121
Sea, Surf & Hills 123
Rainbows & Sky 127
Barometer & Changes 137
Animals, Birds, Insects & Fish 149
Plants 163
Bubbles In Coffee 169
Through The Year 173
Appendix 231
Acknowledgements 244

The Moon, according to the position it occupies in respect to the earth, repeats the influence it exerted on the earth's atmosphere, oceans, and solid crust, when it was previously in a like position; further, it exercises a maximum influence when at a particular angle and in line, or at a tangent, with the sun.

All the details of atmospheric influences repeat themselves at intervals under like conditions of those bodies, and with like conjunctions.

No need exists as to guessing as to what, in such circumstances, will happen. That which has been is that which will be. Nature's own record, made on a preceding day, may be transcribed for tomorrow's use.

Thus, it follows that barometric pressure, increase or diminution of clouds, much or little sunshine, an over plus, an average, or a scanty, supply of rain, earthquake-shocks, volcanic eruptions, will all occur in time come as they did in times past, so long as, in the case of shocks and eruptions, weak spots remain in the earth's crust.

For, it is further demonstrated, that the moon and the sun together control the atmosphere and produce its changes in the proportion of two parts exerted by the moon and one part by the sun.

H.C. Clements, Natural Law in Terrestrial Phenomena, 1890

INTRODUCTION

*Everyone talks about the weather, but
nobody does anything about it.*
                                        -Mark Twain

MORE THAN JUST LORE

The moon has been part of the fabric of our civilisation for thousands of years, so woven into the tapestry of myths and legends and into the dreams and measurement systems of every society that the extent and origin is beyond recorded knowledge. Superstitions still abound, but there are many who swear the old sayings hold truth, and that the overlay of modern science has done little to underrate their use.

Perhaps it is because although the sun has a special place

in our lives, as the giver of light, warmth and solar energy in all its manifestations, it is the moon that has our affection. When we are over the moon we are happy, when we reach for the moon we are ambitious and when we are "moody" we feel sullen and dark.

There are many quaint superstitions concerning the moon. It was once said that when New moon is seen for the first time it should be respectfully greeted with a bow or curtsey in its direction, and if wearing a hat in the Moon's presence, it should be doffed for a moment. Bowing three or nine times, wishing during the process, was also done. In fishing villages children would recite a charm to keep their sailing fathers safe: 'I see the Moon and the Moon seas me, God bless the sailors on the sea'.

It was always customary to turn over silver in one's pocket upon first seeing the new moon, as this meant there will be plenty of money during the coming month, and many people still do this today for luck. In some districts a special coin was carried and turned over three times when the new moon was seen. To be without any coins to turn over, however, was unlucky.

The waxing and waning of the moon gave rise to many beliefs about the timing of events. It was formerly believed that animals should not be slaughtered while the moon was waning, as the meat would shrink more during curing and cooking. Anything cut during the waning moon would not grow again, or would grow abnormally slowly, so corns were often pared at this time, and hair which was meant to stay short would be cut. A child born under a waning moon was purported to be weak or unlucky all its life, and animals born during the moon's wane would not thrive as well as those born under the waxing moon. Marriages celebrated under a waning moon were deemed to be unhappy and possibly barren, no doubt stemming from the ancient connection between the moon and fertility. On the other hand, the waxing moon was far more fortunate. Hair trimmed during the waxing moon would grow thick and lovely; eggs set under a hen then would not go bad, and seeds planted during a waxing moon would thrive.

The word 'lunacy' derives from the Moon, which was once believed to cause madness. Sleeping in moonlight was once said to be dangerous because it led to lunacy, blindness or some other serious disorder.

Warts could be cured by blowing on them nine times at the full moon. Another wart remedy was to catch the rays of the moon in a metal bowl (preferably silver) and go through the movements of 'washing' one's hands in the rays while saying:

'I wash my hands in this thy dish, Oh man in the Moon, do grant my wish; And come and take away this'.

There was once a wide belief that cutting or burning ferns brought rain, and in some districts this also applied to heather. Other rain-bringing methods included sprinkling water on stones whilst reciting a charm, or tossing a little flour into a spring and stirring with a hazel-rod. In mediaeval times images of the saints were often dipped into water during a drought.

Children's charms to drive away rain are still common today, the most famous being 'Rain, rain, go away, come again another day'. A variant on this charm offers to bribe the rain to go:

'Rain, rain, go away
Come again tomorrow day
When I brew and when I bake
I'll give you a little cake.'

Rainwater was believed to have healing properties when it fell on particular days, especially Ascension Day, or rain that fell at any time during the month of June. The water must be collected after falling directly from the sky; rain which ran off leaves or off the roof was useless. A Welsh belief was that babies bathed in rainwater talked earlier than others, and that money washed in rainwater would never be stolen.

Some superstitions are based on fact and some on fear. Occasionally science and religion have strayed into each other's territory. The only guide is which rules and instructions have stood the tests of time. Although we think that we live in technologically advanced times, science still has not investigated the moon's behaviour fully. Astronomy continues to focus mainly on invisible planets millions of light years away, and in so doing still largely ignoring the moon, our nearest celestial neighbour. Accordingly, still not much is known about its motion or its effect on Earth. This is surprising in a modern age that prides itself on scholastic achievement. The problem is partly the history and development of religion, and because the moon was always the symbol of pagan worship it began to be marginalised as the new Order slowly replaced what went before. Nevertheless the moon is still there two millennia later, and whatever powers and special energies it once had, if it ever did, must be present still.

Before satellite weather pictures, before accurate measuring instruments such as the barometer, the thermometer, the anemometer, the rain gauge, the hydrometer and before the position of Weather Forecaster had been thought of, most people worked in the open and observed the weather every day. These people observed patterns in the weather, and as they discussed these patterns with friends and neighbours rhymes were developed to assist them to remember each pattern. The rhymes assisted then to pass the information on to the next generation.

The rhymes found in this book have endured generations quite simply because they have proved to be true over and over again. They were developed by different groups of people: the sailor/fisherman; the farmer/shepherd and the general community. We often find the same theme with slightly different words. The length of time that these rhymes may have existed is perhaps illustrated by an article in Readers Digest of September 1988 titled "Viking ships hoist sail again".

In Skuldelev, a village on the Roskilde Fjord just west of Copenhagen, legend had it that a ship had been sunk in the navigable channel of the fjord, in the early 1400's, to block enemy passage to Roskilde. In 1956 a well preserved boat's rib was recovered, and found to be much older than believed, dating back to around AD 1,000. In all five ships were recovered.

This legend had been passed on by word of mouth for nearly 1000 years without any visual assistance:

Red sky in the morning, shepherds warning.
Red sky at night, shepherd's delight.

It appears in the Bible in the following, less alliteral form:

...He answered and said unto them, "When it is evening, ye say, it will be fair weather: for the sky is red. And in the morning, It will be fair today: for the sky is red and lowering.

(Mathew 16:3)

For more versions of this one, see Chapter 15. There is every reason to believe that this proverb is even older than 2,000 years, as much of the Bible is known to have been imported in great chunks from earlier Egyptian, Babylonian and Sumerian texts. Egypt was known to have been settled 600,000 years ago, and the Great Pyramid may be up to 300,000 years old or older.

The weather is on view every day, so it is very possible

that many of the rhymes in this book's collection also could be more than 2,000 years old. They have appeared in writings of Theophrastus, Aristotle, Pliny, Cicero, Didonus, Virgil and others; in farmers' catalogues, and in old almanacs where scientists, poets, philosophers and teachers have set down rules for daily living. That they reached the present day is an indication of which may have survived the test of time.

There have always been scientists, philosophers and observers who have fervently believed the moon is responsible for our weather, and in the larger patterns of its orbiting behaviour; our climate. A planetary body between a third and a quarter the size of our own in close proximity to us surely must affect our atmosphere. It would be more bizarre if it didn't - add to that its moon's inconstancy and you have a powerful agent to be continually mixing the climatic environment.

Although the Egyptians purportedly had telescopic lenses, as evidenced from pictures on hierographs, Copernicus and Galileo were among the first in modern times to build modern telescopes to examine the moons of planets such as Jupiter and declare that moons obviously affected their host planets. Current studies of the over 50 known planetary moons have shown that planets with moons, such as Mars, have unstable weather compared with planets without moons like Venus that have relatively unchanging weather. The rule seems to be, if you have a moon, you have changing weather.

As the sun sets and we prepare to retire for the day, the moon is often just beginning its appearance in the sky and when above us it dominates the night. Perhaps it has been with the introspection that often accompanies darkness that we have looked to the moon for guidance and wisdom. Much of that guidance would have been for sound decisions in agriculture, and man probably noted time and again that the look of the moon often preceded the same weather developments. Weather folklore was born.

Years later connection between lunar phases and the

weather has sometimes been seen as mere lore. Today we expect science to solve the riddles in nature quite forgetting that science was and still is deeply rooted in simple observation. For early civilisations though, science was the knowledge of the gods themselves, in a process whereby the elemental factors were given human names and worshipped as a child would worship a parent. Early answers to these riddles and enigmas took the form of myths, legends and proverbs.

Perhaps the reluctance to embrace them today is due in part to our inherited form of them, because invariably they are quaint and simple images in hues picturesque and nostalgic. Some, when found not to work 100% of the time are thrown away and dismissed as 'old wives tales', yet when the forecasters get it wrong on TV we apply a different rule standard and tend not to treat them as harshly.

THE MOON AND LIFE

Life evolved after the moon made weather, tides, and the rotation of the Earth possible. The future is forecast that as the moon moves away from Earth, Earth will slow and cease to rotate, the weather system will fail, and life as we know it will perish as the earth settles into frozen or baked wastelands.

The moon is known to play a vital role in sustaining and monitoring planet Earth. Without the moon there would arguably be no life, because the ever-changing atmosphere ensures that warmth is distributed through the night to all parts. Otherwise, with the sun as the only celestial being, the dark side of the earth each night would freeze to minus 220degrees F and nothing could survive. By day, there would always be one large cloud facing the sun, no sun's rays would get through, plants would not photosynthesise and so no oxygen could be produced.

That is why it is wishful thinking and a little unscientific to assume there is a high chance of life on other planets, especially in a humanoid form such as our own species. The moon controls our life-giving atmosphere, our energy levels, the tides that control all sea-life which feed a large portion of humanity, and many hidden aspects to our daily living such as endocrinal cycles such as menstruation-ovulation, which is the major part of the way we continue to reproduce and so survive as a species.

Therefore when looking for evidence of life on other planets we should be looking for planets with a moon just like ours, with the same sizes and distance away as in our own Earth/Moon situation. This search should also involve a planet/moon system the same distance from the sun star which has to be the same as our sun star, or the gravity and radiation levels would be prohibitive for life as we know it. But this severely narrows down the search possibilities and the chance of ever finding such a situation, in fact about as much chance as finding two leaves, raindrops or human faces that are absolutely identical. Perhaps it is better for the ongoing funding of astronomical research to let everyone believe otherwise.

THE MOON AS MEASURER

The moon's role as a god enshrined it as an unfailing measurer of time. Indeed, the very word itself, 'measure' is derived from moon, as is month and metre; and series and sequence derive from Selene, the Greek name, and from where the Romans derived 'Luna'.

It did not escape the attention of our forefathers that the effects of countless activities were subject to particular rhythms in nature. Operations and medications carried out on certain days were successful but proved useless at other times, quite regardless of dose, quality and skill of the practitioner, fisherman or farmer.

Numerous buildings of the ancient Egyptians, Greeks,

Romans, Indians and Babylonians testify to the importance placed on the observation of heavenly bodies and the exact calculation of their movements. Insights into the congruencies of seasons, weather and positions of stars joined into a tool well suited for future prediction.

Stone circles were erected to keep track of the moon, sun and constellations. Some, like Stonehenge, were huge and dimensionally intricate, whilst many such as those around Lands End were simple affairs. Yet all were built to the same plan and, now decoded, reveal a predominantly lunar focus. Their construction would have been needed because a society totally dependent on agriculture would have called for weather and climate calculators and personnel, just as we do today.

Thus sun, moon and stars were transformed into the hands and face of a celestial clock. Shamans, mindful of the mathematics and possessing of the secrets, would, as shamans still do today, calculate the time of rains and organise the prayer meetings and rain dances just beforehand. The ensuing rains would have been seen as answers to prayers and the rule of the political and religious elites were reinforced.

In some cases, whole hills were carved as shadow-dials, so afternoon shadows viewed from certain angles told of nearness to equinox or solstice. Such hills are still to be found in NZ, parts of England and Egypt.

CHANGES

THE FALL INTO DISUSE

In the course of a few centuries the knowledge about the influences indicated by the positions of the moon fell into oblivion, so much so that people today who do not live out in the elements react with sceptical astonishment and suspicion when a weather role for the moon is claimed.

Those farmers, fishermen, trampers, sailors, surveyors etc. who do live a rural life have remained in touch, so much so that the ability to predict rain and to anticipate dry spells simply by the observations of the different colours and formations of the moon has been kept alive. The Farmers Almanac has evolved from such observations and has been for many a year a trusted and valued reference guide for forecasting weather predictions, understand positive gardening aspects, breeding, fishing and other Lunar aspects.

Today some lore and many lunar phase weather connections have been validated through scientific research.

The new moon holds the old moon in its arms, and this foretells fair weather.
In fair weather conditions the air is of a higher pressure, drier and more stable, which minimizes turbulence. This lack of turbulence allows us to see

more dim objects in the sky than we would see in more unstable conditions. Since a stable air mass is typically associated with fair weather the statement holds true.

So, if you look at the New moon and can see the outline of the remainder of the moon which is in shadow, you *can* expect fair weather to arrive soon. The circle that you can sometimes see around the moon is caused by refraction of light through ice crystals. These ice crystals are quite high in the troposphere and are usually associated with a thin layer of cirrus clouds. Often this layer of ice crystals will precede a developing storm by 24 to 36 hours. The circle does not mean it will rain or snow, but it can be an indicator that there may be a chance of precipitation in the next couple of days.

Research has linked hurricanes to the Full and New Moon's with data collected. Data has also shown that rainfall is more likely to occur at the First Crescent that at the First Quarter of the Moon, and at the Disseminating Moon phase rather that at the Third Quarter. Records also suggest that more rain seems to occur during the two weeks of the waxing Moon that in the night after the Full Moon.

THE HERSCHEL TABLE

The classic American almanac weather table, also called the Herschel, was named after the astronomer-royale Sir William Herschel who devised this particular methodology to predict the weather long-range so he could arrange for his observing sessions with telescopes. It was taken up by farmers in Europe and found its way into the New-England Farmer's Almanac for 1854, the Farmer's Almanac for 1855, and *Poor Richard Revived* for 1914, foretelling the weather throughout all the lunations of each year. It is said that Sir John Herschel, late in his life, disavowed any connection to the chart.

FINDING THE EXACT TIME OF PHASE CHANGE

The Herschel Chart takes the time of the change of moon phase and converts it to a prediction of the weather for the next several days after the moon changes phase. The exact time of the change of phase is often printed in daily newspapers, or is available in ephemeris charts and from astrological sites on the internet, free on:
http://www.starlight.demon.co.uk/mooncalc/
http://www.newageinfo.com/lbin/phoon
http://www.sarum.com/moonviewer.html

Or purchasable at:
http://www.astrologyware.com/janus3/support/faq.shtml

HERSCHEL'S WEATHER TABLE

This table, about 400 years old and once very popular with farmers, shows the observer what kind of weather will most probably follow the entrance of the Moon into any of its quarters, and claimed to be 'so near the truth as to be seldom or never found to fail'. If the New Moon, First Quarter, Full Moon or Last Quarter falls at a certain time of day, the weather will be as follows:

TIME	*IN SUMMER*	*IN WINTER*
12:00am – 2:00am	Fair.	Frost, unless the wind is a south-westerly.
2:00am – 4:00am	Cold & showers.	Snowy & stormy.
4:00am – 6:00am	Rain.	Rain.
6:00am – 8:00am	Wind & rain.	Stormy.
8:00am – 10:00am	Changeable.	If westerly winds, cold rain. If easterly, snow.
10:00am – 12:00pm	Frequent showers.	Cold & high winds.
12:00pm – 2:00pm	Very rainy.	Snow or rain.
2:00pm – 4:00pm	Changeable.	Fair & mild.
4:00pm – 6:00pm	Fair.	Fair.
6:00pm – 8:00pm	If north-westerly winds, fair.	If northerly or north-easterly, fair & frosty.
8:00pm – 10:00pm	Southerly or south-westerly winds, fair.	If southerly or south-westerly, rain or snow.
10:00pm – 12:00am	Fair.	Fair & frosty

OBSERVATIONS

1. The nearer the time of the Moon's change, first quarter, full and last quarter are to *midnight*, the fairer will be the weather during the next seven days.

2. The space for this calculation occupies from ten at night till two the next morning.

3. The nearer to *midday* or *noon* the phases of the Moon happens, the more foul or wet weather may be expected during the next seven days.

4. The space for this calculation occupies from ten in the forenoon to two in the afternoon. These observations refer principally to the summer, though they affect spring and autumn nearly in the same ratio.

5. The Moon's change, first quarter, full, and last quarter happening during six of the afternoon hours – *i.e.*, from four to ten – may be followed by fair weather; but this is mostly dependant on the *wind*, as is noted in the table.

6. Though the weather, from a variety of irregular causes, is more uncertain in the latter part of autumn, the whole of winter, and beginning of spring, yet in the main the above observations will apply to those periods also.

7. To prognosticate correctly, where the *wind* is concerned, a *vane* should be in sight.

WEATHER INDICATIONS

SUNSET COLOURS. – A grey, lowering sunset, or one where the sky is green or yellowish green, indicates rain. A red sunrise, with clouds lowering later in the morning, also indicates rain.

HALO (SUN DOGS). – By halo we mean the large circles, or parts of circles, about the sun or moon. A halo occurring after fine weather indicates a storm.

CORONA. – By this term we mean the small coloured circles frequently seen around the sun or moon. A corona growing smaller indicates rain; growing larger, fair weather.

RAINBOWS. – A morning rainbow is regarded as a sign of rain; an evening rainbow, of fair weather.

SKY COLOUR. – A deep blue colour of the sky, even when seen through clouds, indicates fair weather; a growing whiteness, an approaching storm.

FOG. – Fogs indicate settled weather. A morning fog usually breaks away before noon.

VISIBILITY. – Unusual clearness of the atmosphere, unusual brightness or twinkling of the stars, indicate rain.

CLOUDS. – In observing clouds we observe their kinds, motions, and outlines. The clouds frequently called "mares' tails" we term Cirrhi. They are marked by their light texture, fibrous and sundered as in the "mare's tail," or interlacing as in the far-spreading white cloud, which produces the halo. Small regularly-formed groups of these clouds are frequently seen in fair and settled weather. The Cirrhi are also the clouds on the forepart of the storm. In this case they are usually more abundant, their outline is very ragged, and they generally blend into a white, far-reaching cloud-bank. The cloud well known as "cotton bales" or "thunder heads" we term cumulus. When they appear during the heat of the day and pass away in the evening, continued fair weather may be expected. When they increase with rapidity, sink into the lower part of the atmosphere, and remain as the evening approaches, rain is at hand. If loose patches appear thrown out from their surfaces, showers may be expected. The clouds usually seen after nightfall, lying in one horizontal plane, and not of great extent, are attendant on fine weather. Small, black, inky clouds and dark scud indicate rain.

BAROMETER. – In using the barometer, we should notice whether it be greatly above or below the mean height, and the rapidity of its rise or fall. If it be higher and steady, continued fair, though not cloudless, weather may be expected. If it be lower and falling, rain, or at least damp, cloudy weather, is at hand. A rapid rise or fall (greater than 0.01 inch per hour) indicates continued unsettled weather and much wind.

CHANGE IN FOLKLORE

When changes of the moon occur in the morning, expect rain.

Moon changing in morning indicates warm weather; in the evening, cold weather.

If the moon is rainy throughout, it will be clear at the change, and perhaps the rain will return a few days after.

If the moon change on a Sunday, there will be a flood before the month is out.
(Worcestershire)

A Wednesday's change is bad.
(North Italy)

A Friday's moon
Is a month too soon.
(Sussex)

A Saturday moon,
If it comes once in seven years, comes once too soon.
Saturday's moon and Sunday's prime
Once is enough in seven years' time.
Scotland)

A Saturday's change and a Sunday's full moon
Once in seven years is once too soon.
A Saturday's change and a Sunday's full
Comes too soon whene'er it wull.
(Dorset)

Saturday's moon, Sunday's seen
The foulest weather there ever hath been.
If the moon on a Saturday be new or full,
There always was rain, and there always wull.
(Worcestershire)

Saturday's change and Sunday's full
Never brought good and never whull.
(Norfolk)

The nearer the full to 12 in the afternoon, the drier the moon. The nearer to 12 in the forenoon, the wetter the moon.
When the new moon comes in at midnight, or within thirty minutes before or after, the following month will be fine.
(Herefordshire)

DAYS AFTER THE MOON CHANGE

So far we have looked at lore indicated the few days' weather around and just after the hour of phase change. But what about for the rest of the month? It was widely believed that what the weather was, within a few days of phase change, signalled the likelihood of weather for the whole of the rest of the month.

A hundred hours after the new moon regulates the weather for the month.
(Huntingdonshire)

From the first, second, and third days of the new moon nothing is to be predicted; on the fourth there is some indication; but from the fifth and sixth days the weather of the whole month may be predicted.
(Marshall Burgland's Motto)

The first and second never mind,
The third regard not much;
But as the fourth and fifth you find,
The rest will be as such.
(Huntingdonshire)

If the new moon is not visible before the fourth day, the air will be unsettled for the whole month.
(Bacon)

If on her fourth day the moon is clear, with her horns sharp, not lying entirely flat, nor standing quite upright, but something between the two, there is a promise mostly of fair weather till the next new moon.
(Bacon)

The prime or fourth day after the change of the moon doth most commonly determine the force and direction of the wind.
(Pliny)

The dispositions of the air are shown by the new moon, though still more on the fourth rising, as if her newness were then confirmed. But the full moon itself is a better prognostic than any of the days which succeed it.
(Bacon)

As is the fourth and fifth day's weather,
So's that lunation altogether
(From the Latin.)

From long observation, sailors suspect storms on the fifth day of the new moon.
(Bacon)

The weather remains the same during the whole moon(month) either as it is on the fifth day if it continues unchanged over the sixth day(eleven times out of twelve), OR as it is on the fourth day if the sixth day resembles the fourth(nine times out of twelve).
(France, article in the Guardian, 2nd of September, 1868)

If the weather on the sixth day is the same as that on the fourth day of the moon, the same weather will continue during the whole moon.
(Spain, said to be correct nine times out of twelve.)

MYTHOLOGY

MOON AND SUN

We will return soon to the weatherlore. First we will look a bit more at the way moon cults spread around the world and how they eventually became suppressed. It is rather a coincidence that the two bright luminaries, sun and moon, appear in our sky as roughly the same visual size, even though one is nearly 400 times further away than the other. Probably for that reason, in ancient times both assumed an equal mythological importance. In most ancient cultures the sun and moon play complimentary or adversarial roles. They were given human personalities and god-names, and both were worshipped equally and assigned equal tasks. Sometimes the hero and villain roles were reversed. Invariably one was always trying to curry favour with the other just as in any human relationship. And as happens often with humans the differences between the two sometimes become exacerbated.

THE TREE OF THE WORLD

An ancient Indian legend tells of heaven and earth linked by a tree, with the moon hiding in the roots beneath the earth's surface. The sun appeared above the earth in the sky amongst the leaves. The moon and sun were seen as brother and sister and incestuous, she spurning his perversity and throwing ashes into his face thus paling his brightness and shaming him from her presence (The Book Of The Moon, Tom Folley).

Myths from central Asia describe a world illuminated by people whose high god stirred the primeval waters so releasing sun and moon to spring into the heavens and take over the duties of providing light. Some tribes describe the moon as shy, moody and elusive, creeping out at night whilst humans slept, and sometimes so shy as to even hide completely.

Other tribes were grateful for the moon's light, as it illuminated the night, especially a Full moon on a winter's night (when the moon is always higher in the sky), whereas it was thought the sun's rays did little to illuminate a day that was already lit.

LATVIA LEGEND

From Latvia comes the story of the moon wedded to the sun but wandering alone in the early morning because the sun refused to rise with her. For her solitary wanderings the moon was cleft with a sword, creating the quarter moons.

GREEKS, ROMANS, CATS

The Greek goddess Selene became the Roman goddess Luna, and when the Roman Empire expanded, so did Luna's attributes and influence. The moon quickly became the symbol of pre-Christian paganism. Cats, central to Greek life and culture to such an extent that the gods were given cat-faces, were lumped into moon mythology too, and moon healing, nearly always by women who were the disseminators of wisdom, was associated with felines. The tradition of witches and cats came from this era, and when things turned nasty with the rise of Christianity, both became demonised.

Witches' cats became black cats and both were subjects of inquisition. The satanising of the moon saw the 'man in the moon' take the form of Cain, accompanied by his dog in the persona of the Devil and with a thorn bush which symbolised the fall from grace.

THE NUMBER 9

The tie up between cats and the moon was reflected in the number 9, considered both the cat's number and that of the moon. One need only think of the tradition of cats having nine lives, the cat 'o nine tails etc. to see how it has persisted to this day. But the number 9 and the moon stretch back to antiquity. The new moon was once the newn moon, newn meaning nine. Pythagoras called 9 the moon's number. Human pregnancy lasts for 9 lunations. The moon's nodal cycle, between maximum and minimum declinations is 9 years each way, the perigee cycle(when the moon is its monthly closest to earth) is 9 years between northern and southern hemispheres. When, during the day it rains, the showers invariably arrive every 9 hours and/or every 9 minutes. It is the same with wind gusts and earthquake aftershocks. The reader may find this hard to believe until actually checking it out!

MALE MOON

In ancient Egypt before the cult of Isis grew, the moon was a male god with a bull as the main image, said to have been formed by a ray of moonlight falling on the flank of a cow. The ritual bull-leaping of the Cretan Bronze Age, 2500-1200BC, was typical of the moon-based religious cult. Other bull cults were represented in the beliefs of India, Egypt and the Near East. The Minotaur(from 'moon')is the half-man half bull tradition from Crete. India's preoccupation with the sacred cow continues to this day. Siva, the reproductive and fertility symbol of the Hindu, is often depicted riding a bull and with a crescent in his hair.

In northern Arabia, a Bedouin tradition tells of a female sun married to a male moon. She is the passionate one and he the passive partner. In her frustrated sexual passion she attacks him leaving wounds visible today as sunspots. her scars are the marks seen on the moon. Going their separate ways, they find sexual union only once per month, after which the moon gradually shrinks in size and potency.

Normally we find a male moon to be the more lustful of the partnership. In another reason to explain diminishment, a Baltic myth has the moon-god Meness married to the daughter of the sun-goddess Saule. The morning star god Auseklis, also a suitor, cuts Meness to pieces.

In Greenland, the sun-goddess Malina is forever chased across the sky by her brother Annigan, who forgets to eat and grows thinner and thinner. He is forced to descend and find food on earth, before resuming his heavenly chase. The name Malina somehow found its way to the Pacific, first to Hawaii as Mahina, where it again became the moon's name. In Samoa the moon is known as Masina, in Tonga Malina and in New Zealand, Maori for moon is Marama.

SOUTHERN MIGRATION

So was there an early migration that found its way from Greenland, through the Northwest passage in the Bering Strait to the northern Pacific, before launching further west? It is also known that Tonga was settled 20,000 years ago and that Tonga had Egyptian-style pyramids as did Western Samoa, where one is today still standing; the Pulemelei Mound. Decoding has revealed that the dimensions used the same sacred geometry in all structures from the UK to the Pacific.

In the fascinating book Ancient Maps of The Sea Kings (by Charles Hopgood) we find evidence of pre-AD mapping of the southern hemisphere. Quite probably these mapping tools were in the hands of Persian and Phoenician mariners, the result of thousands of years of accumulated knowledge of the Persian, Mayan, Sumerian and even Altantean societies.

New Zealand is pictured in these ancient maps, perhaps 2000 years before Abel Tasman, and labelled Los Roccos Insulis. Also pictured is Antarctica with no snow on, meaning the maps were drawn sometime before the last Ice Age. The famous Piri Reis map that surfaced in Turkey in 900AD was one of these, but it is thought that from the style of ornamentation that surrounds it, the Piri Reis was merely a copy of an earlier original, perhaps part of the 75,000 books and ancient documents that formed the Alexandria library and that were destroyed by fire.

In the Piri Reis, maps of South Africa and South America are accurately depicted as they are today, indicating much cartographic skill that became lost, and, like longitude, had to be rediscovered. From these maps it does seem likely that Indo/Egyptian/Europeans did first colonise the Pacific area.

In Polynesian myth, the moon reverts to female gender. The moon was believed to be the first woman, symbolising fertility and femininity. This far into the future it is not certain which culture preceded the other, but it is clear that successive migrations took the same myths and spread them globally.

An Australian aboriginal myth tells of a man chased off the edge of the world by a wild dog. Returning and hungry, he gorges himself on opossums, becoming too fat to move. The dog returns and eats him, finally tossing an arm bone into the sky as a boomerang, where it becomes the crescent moon. Yet 3,000 year old boomerangs also reside in the Cairo Museum.

MOON AND SOULS

For many cultures such as Persian, Greek, Indian and Eskimo, the moon was the first way station for the dead who were on their way home to heaven. One explanation was the increase in moon size around Full moon, thought to have swelled with newly departed souls. This ties in with real observational data today that more people do actually die around the time of the Full moon when compared to the other phases. The Egyptian dead are depicted in scroll drawings and hierographs to have travelled by First Crescent-shaped boat, in the manner of Nile transport and in the case of Eskimos, the kayak.

In the ancient city of Ur, some 5000 years ago, the moon was the city's patron god. The city was destroyed and rebuilt several times, and each time the moon temples were reconstructed. Moon worship continued to be passed to new conquerors and finally to Julian the Apostate, Roman Emperor 331-63 AD, who was nephew of Constantine The Great.

MOON AND TRAVEL

What may have helped to keep moon culture alive were the requirements of navigation. For travellers in the deserts of the Middle East, the moon and stars pinpointed the way. As well as compasses, sextants and astrolabes were employed not only for direction but also to astrologically determine safe time of travel. Even 18th century navigators like James Cook used a lunar plotting system. During a 24 hour period the moon moves anticlockwise about 13 degrees with respect to the background stars, 22 of its own diameters. Its motion past a chosen star every 28 days can be seen and easily measured, and so constructing the sidereal lunar month. Knowing which star was above which latitude at which time of the year and where the moon should be in the sidereal month gave the traveller a fix anywhere on earth (A Key To Stonehenge, by Robin Heath)

The moon became a guide not only in travel, but in the journey that was life itself. As a person journeyed through the month, the moon reflected his moods and needs. A person born during a waxing moon sign (between new moon and Full) was said to be resourceful, versatile, energetic, firm, frank and sanguine, whereas the waning moon personality explained dullness, lack of drive and direction, caution, prudence, thrift, shyness and seclusion. The astrology of personality grew in this era, and the folklore expanded to more facets of the human condition.

THE MOON AND HERESY

The writings of the Egyptians about lunar lore, customs and rituals, theories on the formation of the earth, qualities of the soul, farming almanac information, mysticism and alchemy were spread by the Greeks and then by the Romans as waves of conquest spread through the Near East and Mediterranean. With the decline of the Roman Empire around 600AD the writings were saved by the Arabs who provided the principle sources of magic for the European Renaissance. Witchcraft was opposed by Christianity, which now had arisen from the ashes of the Roman Empire and taken flight on its own throughout Europe. A gender war had also arisen, between the patriarchal church and the old matriarchal body of healers and disciplines.

Also, as the old science was a predictive one based on lunar cycles, there was no longer a place for the new Christian god, who alone was supposed to know what was going to happen. Anyone claiming to be able to predict anything was labelled heretic. Witchcraft went underground and secret societies such as Freemasonry evolved to preserve and promulgate the sacred teachings.

The dark of the moon; the three days when the moon becomes new, was thought to be perilous for earth and prayer and fasting was necessary. Moonless nights were for cleansing rituals and gathering ingredients for spells against enemies and where once the new moon was (and still is in non-Western societies) a time of celebration, now it became associated with evil.

Some of the mathematics of the moon were satanised in order to create distance between the paganism and the New Order. 13 is a powerful moon number because of the moon's 13 orbits per year(52 weeks divided by 4), and the moon's movement around Earth which amounts to 13 degrees per day. The number 13 was declared unlucky, evil, awkward, undesirable. Even today some big hotels choose to have their 14th floor above the 12th.

Another number to get the chop was 6, called by the Greeks the number of the cosmos. Not only lunar, but part of the sacred geometry of the heavens; integral in the old pagan science, 6 was worshipped by mathematicians in its role as the factorial baseline for cosmic measurement. For instance, the speed of the earth is 66,600 mph. The diameter of the moon is 6x6x60 (2,160) miles. The diameter of the sun is 12x12x6,000 (864,000) miles. The distance from earth to moon is 6x60x660 miles, or 60x the earth's radius. The diameter of the earth is 12x660 (7,920) miles. The mean circumference of the earth is 12x12x12x12x1.2 miles. The area of New Jerusalem, the Great City envisioned by Ezekiel, was 666,000 megalithic yards (Ezekiel 40-48). All factor back to 6.

Miles, yards, hours and feet are all part of the ancient order of standards dating back to beyond the Sumerians. The British once had cubit and the reed alongside mile and yard, but like the fathom, those that fell into disuse fell out of common usage. The gram remains a British symbol of weight, an example of a unit of measurement dating way back to the Egyptian 'grain' and the long forgotten time when wheat was only just beginning to be a tradable commodity.

The moon itself was the basic unit of measurement. Weights and standards were linked to the dimensions of the Khafre Pyramid, so-called Pyramid of the Moon. The math of the cosmos was symbolised in everyday transactions in the marketplace. Everything tied together, and by linking to cosmic denominators the knowledge was carried far and wide as trade expanded. For example, by casting wheat onto a portable set of balance scales it was possible to compute in advanced astronomy.

Thousands of years ago a global culture existed, with technology we have no inkling of, and all we have left to view and study of it are enigmatic structures like Stonehenge and the Great Pyramid. We also have the higher mathematics, reflected in the stonework itself. For a detailed description of how the ancient mathematics was utilised, visit the website www.celticnz.co.nz.

The way the moon moves is complicated at first, but once understood it can be readily seen to be in the driving seat as to weather and climate.

CYCLES

MOON DECLINATION

Much folklore refers to weather cycles, and when things come around again. The weather 'turning' probably originally referred to the moon turning, from its northernmost point in the 27.5 day 'declination' cycle to begin its trek again southward. Weather systems slow at this time as the moon's orbit runs parallel to that of the earth for a few days.

> *The moon seems never to cross the equator without there occurring at the same time a palpable and unmistakeable change in the weather. Such changes most commonly are accompanied by either by strong winds, gales, sudden frost, sudden thaw, sudden calms, or other certain interruptions of the weather, according to the season.*
> (Clements, 1864)

When the moon reaches its northern point the winds change and suddenly grow colder, because in a few days' time the moon begins dragging polar air southward. Conversely at the southern declination point, as the moon prepares to travel north again from being nearer the tropics, for the northern latitudes; warm breezes are about to start.

Declination is a large feature of stone circles, whereby the stones have been placed to view the moving moon not only around the year's clock, but also the Grand Lunar Declination cycle of 18.613 years, being the interval between maximum northerly points.

This was important to know, because climate variation occurs over this period. At the minimum declination point, the lower end of the cycle, called Minor Standstill, a run of dry days is typically longer, as is a spell of bad weather. The moon is travelling north and south each month but staying between the tropics. Adding a degree per year to its latitude, and a tilt the other way, after 9 years the moon has strayed outside the topics and requires a greater angular momentum to traverse the earth. At this time dry and wet spells are of a shorter duration. The earth warms because of a larger spread of available atmosphere, and these cycles are mentioned in old literature.

> *During the moon's passage in her orbit from quadratures to syzygy, her action on air currents will increase. conversely, when she has great north declination it ought to be greater here than when she is far south, and when in perigee greater than in apogee.*
> (Fitzroy)

> *Whenever the Moon's declination exceeds the Sun's declination, it will rain.*
> (Boyd)

In the northern hemisphere, summer New moons are in the north and hence are closer to the poles. Winter New moons are at the southern declination and are not as vicious as winter Full moons which are in the north.

The year of the moon is only 355 days, before it is again in position with respect to the background stars. Publious Vergilius Maro was a Roman poet 70-19BC. and the author of the epic poem Aenid. His pen name was Virgil. Under that nom de plume he wrote much on moon, weather, crops and guides to daily living.

> *Observe, the daily circle of the sun,*
> *And the short year of each revolving moon:*
> *By them thou shalt foresee the following day;*
> *Nor shall a starry night thy hopes betray.*
> *When first the moon appears, if then she shrouds*
> *Her silver crescent, tipp'd with sable clouds,*
> *Conclude she bodes a tempest on the main,*
> *And brews for fields impetuous floods of rain;*
> *Or if her face with fiery flushings glow;,*
> *Expect the rattling winds aloft to blow.*
> *But four nights old,(for that's the surest sign)*
> *With sharpened horns if glorious then she shine,*
> *Next day, not only that but all the moon,*
> *'Till her revolving race be wholly run,*
> *Are void of tempests both by sea and land.*
> (Virgil)

> *The moon is the Great Distributor of Clouds and therefore is largely the Controller of Solar Heat. It is idle to say the Moon has no appreciable influence on the weather.*
> (Clements)

NEW MOON IN NORTH

New Moon far in north, in summer cool weather; in winter, cold. If New moon is in north, it will be cold for two weeks.

NEW MOON IN SOUTH

New moon far in south indicates dry weather for a month. If New moon is far in south, it will be warm.

35 YEAR TURNAROUND

They say it is observed in the Low Countries that every five and thirty years, the same kind and sute of years and weathers comes about again; as great frosts, great wet, great droughts, warm winters, summers with little heat, and the like; and they call it the prime: it is a thing I do the rather mention because, computing backwards, I have found some concurrence.

(Bacon's Essays, No.LVIII; *Of Vicissitudes of Things*')

WINDS

In February 2001 it occurred to this author as quite feasible that the tide of the air must behave in a similar fashion to the tide of the ocean. As the body of air 'went out' it must hasten, just as the water does, and when right out, there must be less of it.

I decided that if I could prove the atmospheric tide; given that the low atmospheric-tide (moon below horizon) could be a dangerous time for aircraft, then it might be feasible that two major unsolved air crashes in NZ's history, the 1963 NAC 21-death tragedy in the Kaimai ranges and Ansett 708's fatal crash in the Tararuas could have occurred at some unfortuitous lunar period.

I reasoned that I needed to look at a data sheet containing an hourly wind-direction and wind-speed reading at a location that was devoid of hills and coastal sea. With no hills to alter it, the wind direction would be purer, and an in inland location would be unaffected by the sea tide. I planned to plot these observations against moonrise and moonset times for that location, something easy enough to do with an astronomical computer program such as Janus 2, to see if the wind altered in any appreciable way just during the hours of moon rising or setting. If cause and effect could be inferred, then, like the sea-tide which causes the water to flow in a particular direction and speed when incoming and outgoing, so, too, would the air be subject to a similar exchange, if indeed that air was tidal.

I selected Hamilton Airport as my location, and January 1st 2001 through to March 31st 2001 as my time frame. If there was a pattern it would show up over the course of three whole months, altogether covering 206 moonrises and sets. Accordingly I purchased the data from the local met service and set to working out the local moonrise and moonset times for that location (Hamilton airport)to plot them against.

In all but 10 cases out of 206, the wind *daily altered more during and only during each moonrise and moonset hour.* On some occasions there was a complete lull just for that hour, some showed a new east/west alignment just over that hour, some a decrease or increase in wind speed just over that hour, some a complete wind direction reversal in that hour and some showed an hour of variable confused winds that blew nowhere in particular during the moon-on-horizon time. Each month started with moonrise hours showing an increase in speed, then midway through the month this pattern reversed. The influence of moon on wind was shown to be totally irrefutable. Two other studies at randomly selected times and locations revealed the same results.

As to the hour of the Ansett 708 crash, the location was the Tararua Ranges 16km east of Palmerston North Airport, the day was June 9th, 1995, moonset on that day was at 0337hrs and moonrise was at 1431hrs , making mid-moon at 9.04am. The crash happened at 9am. The wind-speed on that day reached a velocity peak at the airport right at the time of the rising of the moon. This would also have been the case 16km away in the nearby Tararuas. At the time of the crash the wind had increased in speed by 40% over the previous hour. In the hour before the crash the northerly wind had swung 20deg further to the west and at the time of the crash switched back to the north again. The moonrise itself held the wind well to the west and on the following moonset it returned to a northerly aspect. Immediately after moonset on the 10th it switched to blow from due east.

Similar results were obtained for the NAC crash. There was a two-fold increase in wind speed for the mid-moon (IC) position and another, almost as big increase on moonrise. When the crash occurred the wind had just increased by half as much again. It is very clear that moonrise and moonset cause massive wind changes, just over that hour. I was fascinated to later find a confirmation reference in old weather folklore!

ANSETT 708 TRAGEDY, JUNE 9, 1995					
DAY	**MONTH**	**HOUR**	**DIR**	**SPEED**	**MOON**
9th	June	0100	340°	5.1477	
9th	June	0200	340°	5.1477	
9th	June	0300	340°	6.1772	Moonset
9th	June	0400	340°	5.1477	
9th	June	0500	340°	5.1477	
9th	June	0600	330°	3.6034	
9th	June	0700	330°	4.6329	
9th	June	0800	310°	7.2068	IC
9th	June	0900	320°	7.7216	Crash
9th	June	1000	320°	7.2068	
9th	June	1100	330°	8.2363	
9th	June	1200	300°	10.8102	
9th	June	1300	290°	12.8693	
9th	June	1400	290°	13.8988	Moonrise
9th	June	1500	290°	12.8693	
9th	June	1600	290°	11.8397	
9th	June	1700	290°	10.2954	
9th	June	1800	290°	11.3249	
9th	June	1900	290°	11.3249	
9th	June	2000	280°	10.2954	
9th	June	2100	280°	8.7511	
9th	June	2200	290°	7.7216	

9th	June	2300	290°	6.1772	
10th	June	0000	290°	6.1772	
10th	June	0100	300°	5.1477	
10th	June	0200	310°	4.6329	
10th	June	0300	340°	3.6034	Moonset

NAC 708 TRAGEDY, JULY 3, 1963					
DAY	MONTH	HOUR	DIR	SPEED	MOON
3rd	July	0700	160°	7	
3rd	July	0800	140°	8	
3rd	July	0900	160°	12	Crash
3rd	July	1000	160°	16	IC
3rd	July	1100	160°	12	
3rd	July	1200	var	2	
3rd	July	1300	20°	10	
3rd	July	1400	10°	15	
3rd	July	1500	30°	15	Moonrise
3rd	July	1600	40°	13	
3rd	July	1700	50°	10	
3rd	July	1800	40°	13	
3rd	July	1900	60°	8	
3rd	July	2000	60°	7	
3rd	July	2100	50°	9	
3rd	July	2200	50°	9	
3rd	July	2300	40°	9	

Dir = direction wind was coming from.
Spd = wind speed, measured in m/sec
IC= moon at low air-tide point, on the exact opposite side of the earth to the crash sites.

The reader will kindly forgive the exhaustive explanation in these pages, but it has been included to dispel doubt about aspects of wind-moon folklore.

Winds rise at the times of the rising of the sun and the moon. If the sun or moon on its rising cause the wind to drop, it increases afterwards its force.
(Theophrastus (Signs, etc, J.G.Wood's Translation)

There are certain wind-holes or weather holes, i.e. caverns and clefts, which stand to the inhabitants of the Alps instead of barometers. When the wind blows cold from them fine weather may be expected.

Greater winds are observed to blow about the time of the conjunction of the planets(such as new moon)
(Bacon)

The new moon brings strong westerlies, solid at water level.
(Still)

A north wind with new moon will hold until the full.
(United States)

At full moon sailors know to add a little more sail.

The moon scorfs (swallows) the wind.
(Nautical)

This last piece of lore is especially interesting. Anyone who races modern yachts will report that sometimes when the anemometer is spinning at a fast rate, the sails will, frustratingly, not necessarily fill, yet on other times when the same wind speed is evident, there will indeed be a good billowing. This indicates that the volume of the air must be subject to changes, whilst air of varying densities may still blow at the same speed.

When the moon is full, the air density is at a maximum, because of the moon's gravitational pull on the atmosphere. But as the full moon does not rise until sunset, the daylight hours of a full moon time will have minimum air density, because the air-tide is out, or low. At midday of a full moon the moon is on the opposite side of the earth. Hence winds during daylight hours will be relatively lacking in volume, necessitating the extra sail.

Much wind lore has been handed down concerning direction, and this is tied to the moon's ever-hanging declination, or north/south changes per month. The lunar declination cycle is 27.5 days, after which the moon has returned to the same latitude again. Airflows are pulled by the moon's gravitational force, in the direction the moon is travelling. The moon moves about 13 degrees per day and weather seems to as well, from W to E as viewed on a weather map. The moon drags weather systems eastward.

The wind whirleth toward the S, and turneth about unto the N; it whirleth about continually and the wind returneth again according to his circuits.
(Ecclesiastes i, 6)

The moon pulls from different points on the declination cycle. Consider a starting point as being in the S; then mainly, the moon pulls air-flows from the S to all points further N; thence from south-west to the north-east, from north-west to south-east, and to the east. Wind is caused by pressure differences in the atmosphere, or the difference in the mass of air in different places. Where the pressure is high the air will move outwards to an area where the pressure is lower. The pressure differences are created by the moon being at different positions at different times in the month, and taking a larger mass of air with it wherever it goes. It also creates a temperature difference, which determines when the rain will form and fall. When coming from the south and south-west, warm air is being dragged up from the tropics in the northern hemisphere and up from the poles in the southern latitudes. When coming down from the northern declination, cold polar air is being pulled down in the north by the southward-trekking moon, and warm air from the area of the equator is dragged towards the southern latitudes. Air-flows are not necessarily wind, but are the potential for wind. Actual wind is monitored by local features, hills, bays and plains. The sea has an effect too, whereby by friction at the interface between water and air causes water to move with the air and vice versa, which is why the wind can change when the tide turns. It is also the time rain may be shaken out.

DIRECTION REPORTED

The wind direction reported is ALWAYS the direction from which the wind is blowing. For example, if you report the winds as Southerly at 10 mph, that means the winds are coming from the south blowing to the north.

WIND, GENERAL

HIGH TO LOW

Wind blows from where pressure is high to where it is low. With your back to the wind, the low pressure area is on your left.

INCREASING

If the wind increases during a rain, fair weather may be expected soon.

NIGHT

Winds at night are always bright;
But winds in the morning, sailors take warning.

IN AND OUT

> *A wind generally sets from the sea to the land during the day, and from the land to the sea at the night, especially in hot climates.*
> (J.F.Daniell)

> *In by day and out by night.*
> (Abercromby)

ROARING

Wind roaring in chimney, rain coming.

STORMS

Wind storms usually subside about sunset; but if they do not, they will go on for another day.

RIPPLE

> *There is a peculiar rippling of the wind, or broken way of blowing, which is said always to prognosticate heavy rain within a few hours.*
> (Scotland)

WIND AND RAIN

> *When rain comes before the wind*
> *Halyards, sheets and braces mind*
> *But when wind comes before rain*
> *Soon you may make sail again*

> *Showers allay winds, especially if they be stormy; as, on the other hand, winds often keep off rain.*
> (Bacon)

> *Much wind brings rain.*
> (France)

> *No weather is ill, if the wind be still*
> *Always a big blow before the turn of tide.*
> *On the high tide, then you'll see your shower.*
> *When the wind shifts against the sun,*
> *Trust it not, for back it will run.*

UNSTEADINESS

Unsteadiness of wind shows changing weather. A frequent change of wind, with agitation to the clouds, denotes a storm.

> *The often-changing of the wind doth many times show stormy weather.*
> (Wing, 1649)

AT SUNSET

When after a rough and wet day the wind lulls at sundown, the old Devon farmers say 'Us'll have better weather now, for the wind has gone to sleep with the sun.'

SUDDEN

A sudden storm lasts not three hours.

> *The sharper the blast;*
> *The sooner 'tis past.*
> (Charles Wesley)

LATITUDE TENDENCY

Between the Tropics, wind and currents tend westward. In middle latitudes, wind and currents tend eastward. In high latitudes winds and currents tend from the poles towards the equator.

> *"Beyond 40° south there is no law.*
> *Beyond 50° south there is no God."*

HEAT

> *Great heat brings wind.*
> (China)

OF SUN

> *The heat of the sun on its increase is more disposed to generate winds; on its decrease, to generate rain.*
> (Bacon)

WHISPERING

The whispering grove tells of a storm to come.

VEERING AND BACKING

A veering wind will clear the sky, a backing wind says storms are nigh.

DIRECTION OF WIND

North wind cold,
East wind dry,
South wind warm and often wet,
West wind generally rainy.
(Bacon)

The east-north-east and west-south-west are chiefly wet
North-west, north-north-west and west-north-west bring hail
North-north-east, North and north-west bring cloud
South, west, and east-south-east bring heat.
All other winds drive the clouds before them; the east-north-east alone draws them toward itself.
(Greece) Theophrastus (J.G. Wood's Translation)

North winds bring hail, South winds bring rain,
East winds we bewail, West winds blow amain;
North-east is too cold, south-east not too warm,
North-west is too bold, south-west doth no harm.
The north is a noyer to grass of all suites,
The east a destroyer to herb and all fruits;
The south, with his showers, refresheth the corn;
The west to all flowers may not be forborne.
The west, as a father, all goodness doth bring;
The east a forebearer, no manner of thing;

The south as unkind, draweth sickness too near;
The north, as a friend, maketh all again clear.
(Tusser)

When the wind south-west
Under the cloud blows low,
Field-flowers wax their best,
Fain to be glad and grow.
But when east and by north
The stark storm strongly blows,
Speedily drives he forth
All beauty from the rose.
So with a stern needs-be
The north blast doth dash
And beat the wide waste sea,
That it the land may lash.
(King Alfred) (M.F. Tupper's Translation)

AMERICAN-INDIAN SAYINGS

Wind from the north: cold and snow.

Wind from the river of the north land (north-west): snow.

Wind from the world of waters (west): clouds.

Wind from the southern river of the world of waters (south-west): rain.

Wind from the land of the beautiful red (south): lovely odours and rain.

Wind from the wooded canyons (south-east): rain and moist clouds.

Wind from the land of day (east), it is the breath of health, and brings the days of long life.

Wind from the lands of cold (north-east) brings the rain before which flees the harvest.

When the wind is in the North
Hail comes forth.
When the wind is in the West,
look for a wet blast.
When the wind is in the South,
The weather will be gude.
When the wind is in the East,
Cold and snaw come neist.
(Scotland)

Wind East or West
Is a sign of a blast;
Wind North or South
Is a sign of a drought.

STORM

If the wind is from the north-west or south-west, the storm will be short; if from the north-east, it will be a hard one; if from the north-west, a cold one; and if from the south-west, a warm one. After it has been raining some time, a blue sky in the south-east indicates that there will be fair weather soon.

THE NORTH WIND

A north wind is generally cold and wet because it comes from the north pole, over the sea. It often carried a reputation for cleaning things out. It is said to make men more cheerful (but women less so), and improve the appetite.

A bleak, bad wind, and a biting frost, and a scolding wife come out of the north.

North wind is said to never last more than three days if it comes up at night and heralds fair, frosty but healthy air. The reason is the northern declination of the moon, starting soon on its trek southward. Dragging air downwards it causes snowdrifts in winter in the far north, especially if the time coincides with a full moon, new moon or perigee. But by the time the wind gets to places like Blackpool it has lost much potency. This is because of the land it must traverse to get there. Although the north wind brings to Scotland and northern parts sleet in winter and in summer often hail, in the south it is more renowned for being cool, fresh but mostly dry.

The north wind doth blow
And we shall have snow
(Denham)

The gold (of the sky) cometh out of the north.
Fair weather cometh out of the north.
(Jon xxxvii, 9)

A north wind is a broom for the Channel.
(Cornwall)

With a north wind it seldom thunders.
Cream makes most freely with a north wind.
The north winds cease ceremonially after blowing an odd number of days-three, five, seven or nine.
(Theophrastus, Signs, J.G. Wood's Translation)

THE NORTH-EAST WIND (POLAR CONTINENTAL)

The nor-easter brings clouds and is not considered a particularly desirable wind. An east/north-east wind is generally cold and dry because it comes from Siberia, over land. When the north-east blows at the surface of the earth, its peculiarity in the northern hemisphere is the formation of clouds that move in the upper currents in the opposite direction. To the Greeks the east-north-east wind was known as Kaikas.

To himself he gathers away, as doth Kaikas the clouds.
Theophrastus (Signs, etc.)

Winds from the land of cold bring fruit of ice. Wind from the right hand of the west is the breath of the god of sand-clouds.
(American-Indian proverb)

The wind from the north-east
Neither good for man nor beast.
(Teonge's Diary, 1675)

If the wind is north-east three days without rain,
Eight days will pass before south wind again.
(Fitzroy)

In the southern hemisphere the north-easterly brings onshore breezes and if persistently for three days or more, then there ensue heavy rains.

If for four days (from the north-east) blew winds of Tamatea, no one went fishing.
(NZ Maori saying)

The north-east airflow can bring a low-level temperature inversion, resulting in cloudy (stratus and stratocumulus) conditions, and it is unlikely that cloud would be sufficiently broken for the viewing of heavenly sights like stars. A relatively small easterly shift in wind direction can bring dry, clear, albeit hazy conditions. With a north-east airflow, cloud is usually widespread, but usually clears with the more easterly shift in the wind.

THE NORTH-WEST WIND (POLAR MARITIME)

The north-west brings a frost, around 40 degrees Fahrenheit and below. A more gentle phenomenon, serving rain showers rather than sleet or hail, it was considered quite benign. After dropping its load it then becomes fine. This is possibly due to it usually forming the side of a clockwise wind direction as the moon descends from the north, a relatively harmless system. A north-west airflow can also bring cool, moist, sometimes unstable air that provides good visibility, convection cloud (cumulus), and a slight risk of showers.

Light north-west airflow: Watch out for large clouds, Strong north-west airflow: Few clouds, with good breaks.

Bringing in the finest weather, the north-west wind was said to improve men's tempers.

> *Do business with men when wind is in the north-west.*
> (Yorkshire)

> *Of all the winds, the north by west, north-north-west, and west-north-west most usually blow against others while still blowing.*
> (Theophrastus)

> *An honest man and a north-west wind generally go to bed together.*
> *When the wind is in the north-west*
> *The weather is at its best;*
> *But if the rain comes out of the east,*
> *T'will rain for 24 hours at least.*
> *North-west wind brings a short storm;*
> *A north-east wind brings a long storm.*
> *North-west is far the best;*
> *North-east is bad for men and beast.*

THE EAST WIND

The east wind was not to be trusted. Typically dry and warm but said to indicate approaching rain, the rain to be more continuous, usually lasting a whole day, the east wind had, as it were, a 'bad attitude.' South and west winds are typically more variable. Some mountains in Scotland were said to be unusually clear in the east wind.

> *In an east wind all visible things appear larger,*
> *In a west wind all sounds are more audible and carry further.*
> (Aristotle, Problems)

Technically, when the winter moon is in the northern declination, and the phase is approaching full, the moon has crossed the equator heading north. The cold air is now mixing with the warm air from the south and turbulence is created which gives rise to thunderstorms. A hoar-frost on an east wind indicated cold for a very long time. The heaviest, tempestuous rains often began with the east wind, with the moon toward the north, the wind gradually veering around to south and then west or a little northwest, when the rain usually ceased.

> *A right easterly wind*
> *is very unkind.*
> *The east wind brought the locusts.*
> (Exodus x, 13)

> *The east wind dried up her fruit.*
> (Ezekiel xix, 12)

> *When the east wind toucheth it, it shall wither*
> (Ezekiel, xvii, 10)

A dry east wind raises the spring.
(Cornwall)

Easterly gales without rain during the spring equinox foretell a dry summer.
(Scotland)

Rain and fine weather when they both get lost, come back on an east wind.
(Wales)

The east wind from the morning of the equinox is rainy; but it brings showers and light breezes.
(Greece)

When the rain is from the east
It is for 24 hours at least.
If a light rain came in with a light easterly wind, it would stay for two or three days
(south-east Coast of Tasmania)

The east wind is a relatively drier wind, more biting and deadly than from other quarters, and if blowing much in the spring, injured fruits by breeding worms. Conversely, the west wind is considered more moist, mild and calm.

When the wind is in the east,
The fisher likes it least;
When the wind is in the west,
The fisher likes it best.
When the smoke goes west,
Guide weather is past;
When the smoke goes east,
Gude weather comes neist.
(Scotland)

PHASE CHANGE

If the moon changes with the wind in the east, the weather during that moon will be foul.

THE SOUTH WIND

Weather systems can become slow-moving when the moon is at its southern or northern declination point each month, because the moon's orbit is parallel to that of the earth at these times. When this is combined with the sun being at or near the solstice position, in June for the north (or December for the south) the tendency for the weather to become stationary for a long period will be increased and even extended a few days should the new or full moon be two or three days away from the solstice position, either before or after that time.

> *The south wind can be sticky, foggy, and not a great collector of clouds. If it lasts or becomes violent, it makes the sky cloudy and brings on rain, which comes on rather when the wind ceases or begins to die away, than when it commences or is at its height.*
> (Bacon)

> *The south wind is the worst for the bodies of men; it dejecteth the appetite, it bringeth pestilential diseases, increaseth rheums; men are more dull and slow then than at other times. beasts also are not to be exempted from these influences.*
> (Worledge, 1669)

The new or full moon can by itself cause weather systems to be reluctant to move onto or away from the country, especially in winter months when an anticyclone is slow moving and a northerly airflow is affecting Britain (or a southerly airflow affecting New Zealand), giving cold bleak weather with snow to low levels.

In other words the two stationary periods will run into each other. In the summer, with anti-cyclonic conditions, these circumstances could be the start of a prolonged dry period, or in the winter and with unsettled weather, it could remain that way for over a week or more.

In the north latitudes, when the moon is in the southern declination point, rain or showers may fall with the moon above or below the horizon, and a deep depression may form, otherwise only light or brief showers.

> *Fair weather for a week with a southern wind is likely to produce a great drought, if there has been much rain out of the south before.*
> (Fitzroy)

> *A southerly wind and a cloudy sky*
> *Proclaim it a hunting morning.*

> *As when the south wind o'er the mountain tops*
> *Spreads a thick veil of mist, the shepherd's bane,*
> *But friendlier to the thief than shades of night.*
> (Homer, Iliad)

> *The south wind rises oftener and blows stronger by night than by day, especially in winter.*
> (Bacon, from Aristotle)

The north of Britain finds the south wind in the same way that the south of Britain finds the north wind; something of a spent force.

> *When the weather's in the soud,*
> *The weather will be fresh and gude;*
> *When the wind's in the east,*

Cauld and snaw come neist.
(Scotland)

When the wind is in the south,
It blows the bait into the fishes' mouth.

The winter full moon is always in the north and the winter solstice sun is in the south. The south wind will be mostly when the moon is moving toward the north around First Quarter. Most rain will be from midnight to midday, because the moon is out of the sky then, leaving a depleted atmosphere; the low air-tide situation. The rain and wind will be early in the day.

Towards the end of the year and the beginning of winter, if the south wind blow first and be succeeded by the north, it will be a severe winter.
(Aristotle, Prob.)

THE SOUTH-EAST WIND (TROPICAL CONTINENTAL)

The south/south-east wind is generally hot and dry because it comes from the Sahara, over land. It typically bringing conditions fair, then cloudy, then rain from the west. In Scotland the rain that comes from a south-east wind is expected to last for some time. A south-east airflow is even less likely in August. It would bring fine, dry, hot and hazy weather, with cumulo-nimbus (thunder) clouds later in the day. Generally the south-east airflow brings good conditions everywhere.

The cliffs and promontories of the shore appear higher and dimensions of all objects seem larger when the southeast wind is blowing.
(Aristotle)

THE SOUTH-WEST WIND (TROPICAL MARITIME)

A south-west wind is generally warm and wet because it comes from the tropics, over the sea. Such weather is characterised as overcast, cloud, drizzle, fog, warm. A south-west airflow brings warm, moist, stable air. Light south-west winds provide a threat of fog and occasional cloudy skies (stratus and stratocumulus). Fog is likely to invade low-lying areas.

Light south-west airflow: fog on low-lying, north and west coasts.

Strong south-west airflow: fog on higher south areas

If the south-west blows at the time of equinox, it indicates rain.
(Theophrastus)

*A south-west blow on ye
And ye blister all over.*
(Shakespeare-Tempest)

*Three south-westers, and one heavy rain.
In fall and winter, if the wind holds a day or more in the south-west, a severe storm is coming; in summer the same may be said of a north-east wind.*

The third day of south-west wind will be a gale, and wind will veer to north-west between 1 and 2 a.m. in winter, with increasing force.
(Fishermen of North Carolina)

*In Southern Indiana a south-west wind is said to bring rain in 36 hours.
When the wind shifts to the S and south-west expect warm weather.*

If the wind is south-west at Martinmas,
It keeps there till after Christmas.
Expect a gale from the south-west when after a stiff breeze there ensue a dead calm and drizzling rain, with a fall in the barometer.

THE WEST WIND

A bringer of squalls, thunderstorms, hail, but then the W wind becomes fine. From the Atlantic, a north-west brings brief snowfalls. In Guernsey, the wind direction in summer is likely to be from the west, and the airflow affecting the islands' weather is most likely to be either Polar Maritime (from the north-west) or Tropical Maritime (south-west), rather than Polar Continental (north-east) or Tropical Continental (south-east).

Do business with men when the wind is from the westerly, for then the barometer is high.
The west wind is short-lived.
A west wind, north about,
Never hangs lang (long) out.
(Scotland)

When the wind is in the west, the weather is always best.

Wind west,
Rain's nest.
(Devon)

When wind is west
Health is best.
A west wind carrieth water in his hand.
The west wind is a gentleman and goes to bed (drops) in the evening.

The west wind is the attendant of the afternoon, for it blows more frequently than the east wind when the sun is declining.
(Bacon)

WIND CHANGES

NORTH TO SOUTH-WEST

If wind in daytime shifts from north to south-west or south, rain is pretty sure to follow; if, on the other hand, it shift from south or south-west to north, the weather will probably clear up.
(Devon)

WINDS AT SUNSET

If in unsettled weather the wind veers from south-west to west or north-west at sunset, expect finer weather for a day or two.
(Fitzroy)

NORTH TO NORTH-EAST

If the wind veers from north to north-east, intense cold follows.
(Dove)

NORTH-EAST TO EAST

When the wind turns from north-east to east, and continues two days without rain, and does not turn south the third day, nor rain the third day, it is likely to continue north-east for 8 or 9 days, all fair, and then to come to the south again.
(Fitzroy)

SOUTH TO NORTH

If the wind shifts from south to north through west, there will be, in winter, snow; in spring, sleet, in summer, thunderstorms, after which the air becomes colder.
(Dove)

NORTH-EAST TO SOUTH-WEST

It is a sign of continued fine weather when the wind changes during the day so as to follow the sun.

NORTH TO SOUTH-WEST OR SOUTH

Rain sure to follow.

SOUTH TO SOUTH-WEST OR NORTH

Weather will probably clear up.
(Devon)

NORTH TO SOUTH, SOUTH TO NORTH-WEST

The wind usually turns from north to south with a quiet wind without rain, but returns to the north with a strong wind and rain. The strongest winds are when it turns from S to N by W.
(Fitzroy)

NORTH TO NORTH-EAST

If the wind beers from N to north-east in winter, intense cold follows.
(Dove)

WHEN TO GO FISHING

Fishermen in anger froth
When the wind is in the north;
For fish bite the best
When the wind is in the west.

WINDS FOR FISH

Salmon, sea trout, brown trout: North-west, south, south-west or south-east.

When the wind is in the north,
The fish to bite are loth;
When the wind's in the south
They come with open mouth;

When the wind's in the east;
They won't bite in the least;
When the wind's in the west,
'Tis when they bite the best.

WIND SPEED

MPH	SIGNS
25-31	Large branches moving. Whistling in overhead wires.
32-38	Whole trees moving. Inconvenience in walking against wind.
39-46	Small branches (twigs) break. Impedes walking.
46-54	Slight structural damage. Larger branches, and weak limbs may break.
55-63	Moderate structural and tree damage.
64+	Heavy to severe tree, and structural damage.

THE BEAUFORT WINDS SCALE

BEAUFORT NUMBER	WIND SPEED (MPH)	
0	<1	Calm. Smoke rises vertically, water looks like a mirror.
1	1-3	Light air. Smoke drifts, ripples but no crests.
2	4-6	Light breeze. Wind felt on face, leaves rustle. Small wavelets, crests don't break.
3	7-10	Gentle breeze. Leaves and twigs in constant motion, flags extend, large wavelets, crests break, 'white-horses'.
4	13-18	Moderate breeze. Dust rises, small branches move. Longer waves, frequent white-horses.
5	19-24	Fresh breeze. Small, leafy trees sway. Moderate waves, chance of spray.
6	25-31	Strong breeze. Large branches move, telegraph wires whistle, large waves, white foam and spray.
7	32-38	Near gale. Whole trees in motion, hard to walk. Sea heaps up and white foam blown in streaks.
8	39-46	Gale. Twigs break off trees, waves about 5 metres high.
9	47-54	Strong gale. Damage to chimneys and roofing. Waves 7 metres high, spray effects visibility.
10	55-63	Storm. Trees uprooted. Sea white, heavy, and shock-like. 9 meter waves.
11	64-72	Violent storm. Seldom over land. Waves hide medium-sized ships, foam everywhere.
12	73+	Hurricane. Sea completely white with driving spray.

WHEN RAIN OR SNOW

HOUR OF THE DAY

It will be found that rain, if about, falls mainly at certain times: around the hour of moonrise, the hour of moonset, and the mid-moons in between, being mid-heaven (MH), or when the moon is directly overhead, and IC position, which is when the moon is directly under our feet on the opposite side of the earth to where we happen to be standing. The latter is the most common. As well, there are the 3-hour intervals between these as well, but not as often.

If it is raining it will stop at high tide, as one will know if they lives near the sea, and if it isn't raining and rain is about, it may start then. In other words, it will change do what it's not doing. These are the rules by which the moon, tide and weather seem to work. There is also a 9 factor. When it is a rainy period, the rain will come at 9 hour or 9 minute intervals. So will earthquake aftershocks after an earthquake. If you look up any of the famous earthquakes, like El Salvador, you may find this is so. And for moonrise and moonset , it will be found that the wind gets stronger in that hour also. Alternatively if it was blowing at strength it may cease then temporarily.

The moon travels east. It only appears to go to the west because earth revolves to the east faster beneath it. Every day that the earth moves through 360 degrees the moon has moved further east by its 13 degrees. It is noticeable that the moon moving east 13 degrees per day is about the same rate as the weather moves east across the weather maps from day to day. This is because the moon is pulling the weather systems in that direction. If one gets a shower at say 4pm one day, then chances are that the next day it will be slightly later(about 48 minutes later)because the moon has moved just that little bit ahead.

It is exactly the same reason that tides are a little later from one day to the next. We all accept that the moon pulls the oceans, so just think how much easier it would be to pull the air. If the air has mass then it will be acted on by gravitational forces. The mass of the air? The atmosphere weighs five thousand million, million tons, so yes indeed. The air-tide ebbing and flowing results in the weather.

The atmosphere doesn't move at all unless the moon moves it. Gravity does its best to hold our bit of atmosphere to us as we revolve. The moon's gravity tries to pull the body of air in the direction of the moon

WHEN RAIN IS COMING

When the distant hills are more than usually distinct, rain approaches.

If smoke goes up - clear, smoke comes down - moisture on the way.

When Windows won't open,
And the salt clogs the shaker,
The weather will favour
The umbrella maker!

The further the sight, the nearer the rain.

If the land appears dark from the sea, the wind will be from the west; if light, it will be from the south.
(Theophrastus, Signs, etc, J.G.'s translation)

When the Isle of Wight is seen clearly from Brighton or Worthing, expect rain soon.

When the landscape looks clear, having your back towards the sun, expect fine weather; but when it looks clear with your face towards the sun, expect showery, unsettled weather.
(C.L. Prince)

A mirage is followed by a rain.
(New England)

If the sky is of a deep clear blue or a sea-green colour near the horizon, rain will follow in showers.

A green sky above the sunset foretells rain the next day.

CLEAR SKY

Rain which falls from a fairly clear sky is likely to continue falling in short bursts for some time.

If the moon shows a silver shield,
Be not afraid to reap the field,
But if she rises haloed round,
Soon well tread on deluged ground.

SUN SHOWER

If it rains when the sun shines, it will rain the next day.

LONG FORETOLD

Rain long foretold, long last;
Short notice, soon past.

RAIN RULES

Rain an hour or two before sunrising, likely fair before noon;
If rain sets in by daylight, it will hold up before 8am;
If it begins about noon, it will continue through the afternoon;
If it starts after 9pm, it will rain the next day;
If wind from north-west or south-west the storm will be short;
If storm from north-east it will be a hard one;
If storm from north-west it will be a cold one;
If from south-west it will be a warm one;
If it ceases after 12am, it will rain the next day;
If it ceases before 12am it will be clear the next day;
If it begins about 5pm it will rain through the night;
If raining between 8 and 9am it will go on till noon;
If it doesn't cease then, it will go on till evening.
(Shepherd of Banbury)

RAIN AND WIND

After rains, the wind most often blows to places where the rain falls, and winds often cease when rain begins to fall.
(Aristotle)

WIND STOPPED

> *A hasty shower of rain, falling when the wind has raged some hours, soon allays it.*
> (Pointer)

EAST

> *Rain from the east,*
> *Two days at least.*

SMALL

> *A small rain may allay a great storm.*
> (Fuller)

BULLS

> *Rain, rain pouring*
> *Sets the bulls a-roaring.*
> (Suffolk)

SOUTH

> *Rain from the south prevents the drought,*
> *But rain from the west is always best.*

RAIN DIRECTIONS

WEST

When rain comes from the west, it will not last long.
(United States)

NORTH-EAST

With the rain of the northeast comes the icefruit (hail).
(Zuni Indians)

Rain from the north-east in Germany continues three days.

SNOW

HAY

Much snow, much hay.
(Sweden)

COLD FOLLOWING

In winter, during a frost, if it begin to snow, the temperature of the air generally rises to 32deg, or near it, and continues there while the snow falls; after which, if the weather clear up, expect severe cold.
(Dalton)

THREE DAYS

It takes three cloudy days to bring about a heavy snow.
(New England)

SNOWFLAKES INCREASE

If snowflakes increase in size, a thaw will follow.

STICK

If the first snow sticks to the trees, it foretells a bountiful harvest.

MOON

As many days old as the moon is (since new moon) at the first snow, there will be as many more snows before crop-planting time.

DRY

If the snow that falls during the winter is dry, and is blown about by the wind, a dry summer will follow. Very damp snow indicates rain in the spring.

PHASES AND HORNS

FULL MOON

Each full moon the sky is clearer because the air tide is higher. The atmosphere is effectively stretched which squeezes out low flying clouds. On most full moon evenings the full moon will be seen in all its glory. The evening will be cool because of the lack of cloud. But winds will also drop when the moon gets higher.

In the northern hemisphere winter the Full moon crosses higher, sets further to the north and is in the sky longer than the summer Full moon. The winter New moon sets further to the south, is lower in the sky and is above the horizon for a shorter time. All of these reverse for summer. Midwinter nights have longer moons, a boon for travellers. A frost is more likely on a Full moon night. The US Weather Bureau in 1962 studied patterns of weather occurrence and did find a correlation to phases of the moon. In fact in the seven days surrounding the new moon, rain or snow had a higher probability of falling than during the remaining three weeks of the month. Greek philosophers observed this 2,400 years ago.

The full moon eats clouds.
The full moon grows fat on clouds.
(Nautical)

The weather is generally clearer at the full than at other ages of the moon; but in winter the frost then is sometimes more intense.
(Bacon)

If there be a general mist before sunrise bear the full of the moon, the weather will be fine for some days.

A few days after full or new moon, changes of weather are said to be more probable than at any other time.
(Scotland)

If a change occurs at time of full or new moon, from wet to dry, it will remain fine till the following quarter.

There is a belief that the weather on the fourth, fifth, and sixth days following the new moon during any month, will be indicative of the weather for the following four weeks.

In Western Kansas it is said that when the moon is near full it never storms.

When there are two full moons in one month, there are sure to be large floods.

Near full moon, a misty sunrise
Bodes fair weather and cloudless skies.
If the full moon rise red, expect wind.
The full moon brings fine weather.

If, in the last days of April the full moon come with serene nights and no wind(at which time the dew commonly falls in great plenty), the ancients, from long experience, held it certain that the crops of grain would suffer. The moon has crossed the equator and is heading south, triggering a prolonged dry spell.

If there be a general mist before sunrise near the full of the moon, the weather will be fine for some days.

Threatening clouds, without rain, in old moon, indicate drought.

Auld moon mist
Ne'er died of thirst.
An old moon in a mist
Is worth gold in a kist (chest)
But a new moon's mist
Will ne'er lack thirst.

When it thunders on the day of the moon's disappearance (new moon) the crops will prosper and the market will be steady.
(Assyrian Cuneiform Records, 7th century BC)

FROSTS

Moonlit nights have no clouds to hold in the heat of the day. Clouds hold heat by providing blanket-like cover.

Moonlit nights have the hardest frosts.
Clear moon: frost soon.
(Scotland)

THE EFFECT OF THE AIR TIDE

As the Earth orbits under the moon each 24 hours, in effect, 360 degrees, the moon has only moved 13 degrees across the celestial sky in its orbit around the earth, so when we see the moon going from east to west it is an illusion. The moon travels to the east but because Earth rotates faster beneath it, it appears that the moon travels west. This is akin to travelling in a train and passing a slower train on an adjoining track, which then appears to be moving backwards.

Under the moon at all times there is a bulge of water,

which we call the ocean tides, held towards the moon by its forces of gravitation. As the earth rotates beneath the moon the tide-line shifts to different areas of coastline.

It is the same with the air. A constant bulge of air travels beneath and with the moon. When the moon is above the horizon, rain, if about, is less likely to fall, because the air-tide is high. When the moon sets and disappears over and beneath the horizon the air bulge accompanies it, leaving a depleted atmosphere above the ground. This is the low tide of the air - when the moon is directly beneath our feet and on the opposite side of the earth. The cold of space will come closer to the ground above the horizon at that time; there being no or less atmosphere to keep the cold at bay. Rain, if about, will condense then. If no rain is evident, the air will just get cooler. A good rule is that a moonless sky is more likely to serve rain.

No moon above the horizon can offer showers.
(Alcock)

Birds and bats have a tendency to fly much lower to the ground right before a rain due to the "thinning" of the air, which happens as the moon goes below the horizon. They prefer to fly where the air is the most dense and compacted and they can get greater lift with their wings. With high pressure and dry air, the atmosphere becomes more dense and they can easily fly at higher altitudes. Some references state that birds and bats fly lower to the ground to ease the pain in their ears due to the lowered pressure.

MOON CHANGE

The moon and the weather,
May change together.
A change in the moon,
brings on a change in the weather.

CHANGING PHASE

7 AND 11

New moon is a day moon, rising with the sun and setting with the sun. Rain will come after sunset. A First Quarter moon rises at midday and sets at midnight. Any rain with the moon in 1st Quarter will fall from midnight to the following noon. Hence the following, but it only applies to First Quarter phase.

Rain at seven; fine by eleven
Rain at eight; not fine till eight

MOONRISE AND SNOW

A Full moon will only rise at sunset and set with the sunrise. Full moon cloud or rain will occur during the daylight hours. The Last Quarter moon rises at midnight and sets at midday, so any rain that is about will fall after noon. Snow will fall the most over a New moon or First Quarter period at night, and over a Full moon or Last Quarter during daylight.

If a snowstorm begins when the moon is young, it will cease at moonrise.

This could be referring to the period of New moon to First Quarter.

CROSSING MERIDIAN

During New moon the moon will cross the noon line, the midpoint of the sky. It cannot be seen against the glare of the sun. About two days later it is first visible as a thin crescent in the west after sunset, but only for a few hours. Over a New moon rain is generally not far away, summer or winter. Just after New moon and just after Full are the main times for rain to occur.

If a change of weather occur when the sun or moon is crossing the meridian(noon), it is for twelve hours at least.
(Nautical)

NEW MOON IN THE OLD MOON'S ARMS

On occasion the crescent moon appears with the faint outline of the rest of the moon barely visible. This occurs due to clear, stable and dry air proceeding a high pressure system. It is this clarity that enables you to see the dark part of the crescent moon holding the old moon. This is usually a good predictor of 24 to 48 hours good weather.

To see the old moon in the arms of the new one is reckoned a sign of fine weather, and so is the turning up of the horns of the new moon.
(Suffolk)

Although, others have had alternative views about it:

Late, late yestreen I saw the new moone,
Wi' the auld moone in hir arme;
And I feir, I feir, my deir master,
That we will come to harme.
(Ballad of Sir Patrick Spens)

Like the young moon
When on the sunlit limits of the night
Her white shell trembles amid crimson air,
and while the sleeping tempest gathers might,
Doth, as the herald of his coming, bear
The ghost of its dead mother, whose dim form
Bends in dark ether from her infant's chair.
(Shelley)

MISTS WITH CRESCENT

Mists which occur with crescent moons indicate winds. But those which occur when the moon is doubly convex indicate rain.
(Theophrastus)

CRESCENT HOLDING WATER

It is a common belief that if the crescent is on its back that it resembles a cup or bowl, and the imagination has it that such a bowl can hold water, indicating a wet time coming. This has a simple explanation. When the moon is a thin crescent it is on either side of the new moon. The New moon brings rain, so the crescent indicates rain is probably close by. The light of the moon always points to the sun, so in the course of the day the moon will be seen to revolve as it tracks the sun, either in the sky or wherever it is below the horizon. Also, it will be seen that the crescent is always 'on its back' in early spring, it becomes progressively more upright until early autumn, when it 'stands on its tail.' Then, during the next six months, it slips gradually back to its spring position.

Moon on her back holds water.
(Scotland)

When the moon lies on her back, she sucks the wet into her lap.
(Ellesmere)

If the new moon appears with the points of the crescent turned up, the month will be dry. If the points are turned down, it will be wet. If at her birth, or within the first few days, the lower horn of the moon appear obscure, dark, or in any way discoloured, there will be foul and stormy weather before the full. If she be discoloured in

the middle, it will be stormy about the full; but if the upper horn is thus affected, about the wane.
 (Bacon)

A few days after Full of new moon, changes of weather are thought more probable than at any other time.
(Scotland)

If there be a change from continual stormy or wet to clear and dry weather at the time of the new or full moon, it will probably remain fine till the following quarter, and if it changes not then, or only for a short time, it will probably remain fine and dry for four or five weeks.

If a snow storm begins when the moon is young, it will cease at moonrise.

If mists in the new moon, rain in the old;
If mists in the old moon, rain in the new.
(Shepherd of Banbury)

HORNS SHARP OR DULL

Indistinct outlines of the moon during clear weather betray abnormal inequalities of temperature in successive layers of the atmosphere. Such inequalities are lessened or abolished by strong winds, which often become established in the upper air before they extend to the earth's surface. Hence 'sharp horns' commonly precede a boisterous day.

This and a bright, clear moon are good indicators that wet weather is on the way. As the air clears of dust particles ahead of a low pressure system, the moon appears to become closer and more sharply focused due to the lack of dust.

You may remember a grandparent talking about how their corn, bunions or joints ached right before a rain. This is due to the decreasing atmospheric pressure allowing the gas in our bodies to expand.

A new moon with sharp horns threatens windy weather.

In winter, when the moon's horns are sharp and well defined, frost is expected.
(Scotland)

When Luna first her scattered fear recalls,
If with blunt horns she holds the dusky air,
Seamen and swains predict abundant showers.
(Virgil)

If one horn of the moon is sharp and pointed, the other being more blunt, it rather indicates wind; but if both are so, it denotes rain.
(Bacon)

If the crescent moon stands upright with a north wind blowing, west winds usually follow, and the month will continue stormy to the end.

Whenever the upper horn of the crescent moon stoops forward, north winds will prevail during the period of the new moon; but when the lower horn comes forward, south winds will prevail. But if it is upright, or only very slightly inclined, it is usually stormy till the fourth day; or if the disk of the moon is plainly visible, then until the first quarter. When hazy, it indicates rain, but when fiery, wind.
(Theophrastus, Signs, etc..J.G. Wood's Translation)

If the points of a new moon are up, then, as a rule, no rain will fall that quarter of the moon, a dull, pale moon, dry, with halo, indicates poor crops. In the planting season no grain must be planted when halo is

around the moon.
(Apache Indians)

An erect moon is almost always threatening and unfavourable, but principally denotes wind. If, however, she appear with blunt or shortened horns, it is rather a sign of rain.
(Bacon)

People speak of the new moon lying on her back or being ill-made as a prognostic of wet weather.

New moon on its back indicates wind; standing on its point indicates rain in summer and snow in winter.
(Dr. John Menual)

The bonnie moon is on her back;
Mend your shoes and sort your thack
(Thatch)

If the moon is on its back in the third quarter, it's a sign of rain.

When the moon lies on her back,
Then the sou-west wind will crack;
When she rises up and nods,
Then north-easters dry the sods.
(Symons's Meteorological Magazine, September 1867)

When the new moon lies on her back,
She sucks the wet into her lap.
(Ellesmere)

It is sure to be a dry moon if it lies on its back, so that you can hang your hat on its horns.
(Welsh Border)

MOON SUMMARY

- A clear moon indicates frost.
- A dull looking moon means rain.
- A single halo around the moon indicates a storm.
- If the moon looks high, cold weather may be expected.
- If the moon looks low down, warm weather is promised.
- The new moon on her back always denotes wet weather.
- A double halo around the moon means very boisterous weather.
- If the moon changes with the wind in the east, then shall we have bad weather.
- If the moon be bright and clear when three days old, fine weather is promised.
- When the moon is visible in the daytime, then may we look forward to cool days.
- When the points of the crescent of the new moon are very clearly visible, frost may be looked for.
- If the new moon appears with its points upward, then will the moon be dry, but should the points be downward more or less rain must be expected during the next three weeks.
- If the moon is in the sky, rain is less likely.
- A clear, white moon tells you that the next day will be nice.

ECLIPSES

A battle between two armies on the borders of Turkey in 500AD halted abruptly as a total eclipse began. Thinking it was God's punishment, both sides laid down their weapons, embraced and made a lasting peace.

Christopher Columbus, upset that Jamaican chiefs were withholding vital food supplies to his near-mutinous crew, issued the paramount chief with the threat that if food supplies were not restored, the sun would be taken away. Columbus, as did many mariners of the period, was in possession of almanacs that contained collated wisdom dating from the Greeks, Mayans and Persians. He knew an eclipse was going to occur the following day. As the sun began to disappear the frightened chief consented to Columbus' demands.

An eclipse of the sun was feared by primitive peoples, who worried that the source of light, warmth and light was being devoured forever. From this arose the idea that an eclipse heralded a prominent death or a great disaster such as war, plague or famine. It was believed to be unlucky to view an eclipse directly (as well as bad for the sight).

An eclipse is caused by the Moon crossing the earth's ecliptic, at the nodes. The Moon is crossing the magnetic field lines of the earth, in the manner of a commutator in an electric dynamo. Also the Moon at this time is always full or new and at northern or southern declination. Because of this conjunction of factors, often with a perigee thrown in as well, thunderstorms and fast-moving weather systems could be expected soon; with the arrival of earthquakes, eruptions and/or dangerously higher tides in a few days' time.

Eclipse weather is a popular term in the south of England for the weather following an eclipse of the sun or moon, and it is vulgarly esteemed tempestuous and not to be depended on by the husbandman.

Eclipses may also have been seen as affirmations of the regularity of the lunar and solar cycles. Dr. William Stukeley, who in 1740 was the first to note the summer solstice alignment at Stonehenge, thought that one purpose for the monument may have been to worship 'the serpent.'

Stukeley thought that Stonehenge and similar stone circles had been serpent temples, which he called 'Dracontia.' The idea of the serpent comes from the East, where the moon's nodes were referred to as the dragon's 'head' and 'tail' respectively. Dragons were a concept of fear. Dragon figures adorn ancient oriental art. They are depicted on calendars showing nodal times and warning of dire events.

The key to eclipses is the position of the lunar nodes. Even today, the length of time for the moon to return to a node (about 27.2 days)is called by astronomers the draconic month.

To predict eclipses, knowledge of two other cycles is required. One of these - the length of the lunar month - is easily determined. It is simply the number of days between one Full Moon and the next. This cycle of 29-1/2 days is marked at Stonehenge by two rings of 29 and 30 holes, which together average 29-1/2.

The other cycle, is that of the lunar nodes, the points where the Moon's orbit, which is tilted at a slight angle, intersects the plane of the Earth's orbit.

An eclipse can occur only when the sun is close to being aligned with a node. Because of the increased gravitational pull of moon and sun, together with a lunar nodal crossing, the event *would* have been a signal of foreboding weather, and so eclipse fears were probably well justified.

> *Eclipses of the moon are generally attended by fierce winds, eclipses of the sun by fair weather, but neither of them are often accompanied by rain.*
> (Bacon)

CLOUDS

CIRRUS: THE CLOUD OF CHANGE

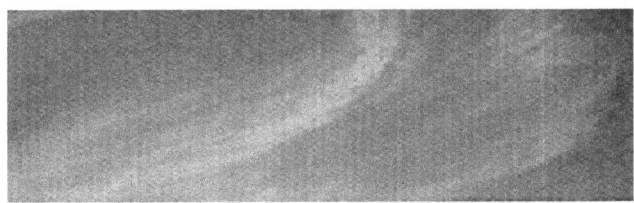

Literally *'curls or tufts of hair'*

After a run of clear or bad weather, the appearance of light streaks of cirrus cloud(mares tails) at great elevation is often the first sign of change. The average speed of cirrus is 70-80mph.

If cirrus curls and wisps dissolve or vanish, fine weather continues. Sheet cirrus occurs mainly with southerly or westerly winds. Murky cirrus may just mean a backing of the wind to an easterly quarter.

Long straight feathery cirrus with soft edges and outlines, or with soft delicate colours at sunrise or sunset, can also be a sign of fine weather.

Rapid cirrus, in distinct dense bars, at right angles to the length of the bars, indicates gale or wind. The bands move transversely and generally precede a storm by twenty to forty-eight hours.
(Hon. F.A.R. Russell)

- The harder and more distinct the outline of cirrus, the worse the weather to come.
- Fibrous, greasy-looking streaks of cirrus with rounded edges or knobs, are a sign of storms.
- Feathery thick patches, equal distances apart denote storms.
- Any appearance of definite waves of alternate sky and cloud, or repetition of the same form, are storm warnings.
- Cirrus in slightly undulating lines are good signs, but deeply indented outlines precede heavy rain or wind.
- Cirrus twisted or zigzag are good; hard and knotted are bad.
- Straight line rays: good , detached patches, bad

When cirrus becomes cirro-stratus, expect change for worse

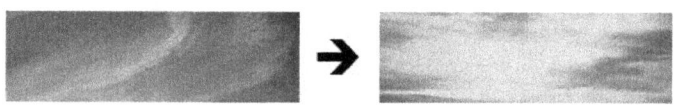

Cirrus announce the east wind. If underside is level and their streaks point upwards, they indicate rain. If downwards, wind and dry weather.

When cirrus is lower and denser than usual, expect a storm from the opposite quarter.

Cirrus from north; settled weather.
Cirrus from east; bad sign in summer, good sign in winter;

Cirrus from south; bad sign in summer, good sign in winter,
Cirrus from west; good sign in summer, bad sign in winter.
Cirrus from south-west; unsettled weather.
Cirrus from north-west, temporary fine weather, especially in summer.

WHEN CIRRUS FORMS A V-POINT:

DIRECTION THE V POINTS	WEATHER
NORTH	Improving weather to the south.
NORTH-EAST	Temporarily settled.
EAST	Settled in winter, disturbances to the south-west in summer.
SOUTH-EAST	Fine in winter, except if after heavy rain, when it indicates squalls. In summer; it means thunder, with damp conditions.
SOUTH	Showery in summer if barometer low; with a high barometer thunderstorms from south-west in summer, and in winter a favourable weather sign.
SOUTH-WEST	Moderately fine.
WEST	In summer, fine to the south and south-east, but unsettled in extreme north-west; in winter, unsettled weather.
NORTH-WEST	Bad sign - indicates sudden fall, with wind and rain.

Goat's hair, or mare's tail forebodes wind. Mare's tails followed by alto-cumulus next day, means rain within twelve hours.

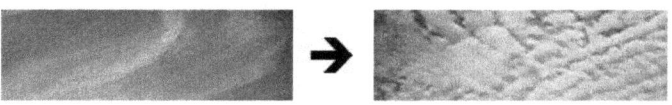

CIRRO-STRATUS:

THE CLOUD OF MAGNETIC DISTURBANCES

Literally 'spread out hair'.

Said to be a sure sign of rain. Continuous cirro-stratus that looks like 'unbroken gloom' presages wind. Waved cirro-stratus indicates heat and thunder.

When cirro-stratus and strato cumulus gather together over the sea: in a line from south-east to south-west, expect rain and probably wind, on the second day.
(C.L. Prince)

If long lines of cirro-stratus are contracted in their centre, expect heavy rain the next day.
(Prince)

Waved cirrostratus indicates heat and thunder.

CIRRO-CUMULUS:
THE CLOUD OF 24 HOUR WARNING.

Commonly called 'Mackerel Sky" Cirro + strato = 'coming storm.'

A mackerel sky denotes fair weather for that day, but rain a day or two after. Before thunder, cirro-cumulus appear as dense and compact masses, in close contact. If soft and delicate in outline, if fleeces gently merge, continuance of fine weather.

If dense, abundant and associated with cirrus, it signifies electrical disturbance often resulting in thunderstorms in summer or gales in winter.

High cirro-cumulus commonly appears a few hours before thunderstorms. The harder and more definite the outline, the more unsettled the coming weather. Moving slowly from north-east, it is a sign of continuance of north-east winds.

Mackeral sky, mackeral sky,
never long wet, never long dry.

A curdly sky,
Will not be twenty four hours dry.

Cirro-cumulus in winter: expect warm and wet weather.

Fleecy clouds all over the sky denote storms, but if they rest on one another like scales; dry and fine.
(Bacon)

Cirro-cumulus in early morning generally leads to a fine and warm day.
(Jenyns)

'Heaven's lambs' driving north-west, indicate continued fine weather.

Both Mackeral and mares tails indicate high winds aloft, often the presence of the jet stream. This in turn usually hints that a cold front is due soon, often with high winds at the surface of the earth. When this happened in the days of sailing ships, the tall-masted ships had to lower their sails a lot to save the masts. The drag of the high winds could topple a tall mast or rip the sails. Lowering their sails would allow them to still use the wind to travel, but would keep the rigging safe from damage.

ALTO-CUMULUS:

THE CLOUD OF COMING THUNDER

Literally 'high piles'.

Also called Cauliflowers, Zeppelins, or flakes. Consists of turret-like upward growths and is composed of water droplets instead of ice. Sometimes these clouds show coloured patches when illuminated by the sun or moon. It is a sure warning of thundery weather. Thicker cloud generally arrives some hours later.

Alto-cumulus often occurs together with altostratus

ALTO-STRATUS:

THE CLOUD THAT CARRIES RAIN AND SNOW

Literally 'high, spread out'

Resembles grey ground glass, covers the whole sky, and when it increases, rain and snow over a wide area, lasting and continuous, may be the result. May also bring drizzle.

CUMULO-NIMBUS:

THE CLOUD THAT RAINS HEAVILY & HAILS

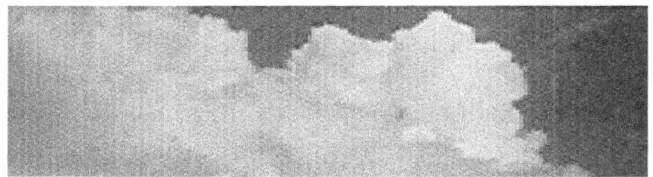

Literally *'gathered piles of rain'*

They are cumulus clouds which are large enough to produce showers. The surest warning of thunderstorms are these clouds, which are in the shape of anvils. They bring thunderstorms, heavy rain and occasionally hail. They can be anything from 1000 to 60,000 feet high.

Towering thunder clouds that look like mountains, early on a summer's day portend intense storm activity during the heat of the afternoon, and often herald torrents of rain in the evening
.(R. Inwards 1945)

When the cumulus rain-clouds look smaller toward sunset than they were at noon, expect fair weather.

The formation of cumulus clouds to leeward during a strong wind indicates the approach of a calm with rain.

Cumulonimbus clouds forming rapidly in the mountains on warm afternoons presage an intense lightning storm is on its way in minutes.

CUMULUS:

THE 'ICE-CREAM' CLOUDS

Literally 'gathering'

Caused by moderate, generally westerly winds. All have a well-defined flat base, between 1500 and 2500 feet high. Cornish fishermen call them 'planets' If they appear early in the morning they will develop into bigger shower clouds. If they do not form till late afternoon they will die away to be followed by a clear sky night. If clouds open and close, rain will continue.

Cumulus high up are said to show that south and southwest winds are near at hand; whereas stratified clouds low down indicate east or north winds.

If the clouds are like fleeces, deep and dense, or thick and close toward the middle, the edges being very white, the surrounding sky bright and blue; they are of a frosty coldness, and will speedily fall in hail, snow or rain.

STRATO-CUMULUS:

THE DOORS TO A COLD FRONT

Literally '*spread out gatherings*'

Large rounded masses or rolls of grey cloud. They cover the sky, sometimes in parallel bands. They usually bring little or no rain. When at sea, the strato-cumulus clouds appear on the horizon, it is a sign that the weather will break up. Being below 8000 feet, stratocumulus can resemble a blurry rippling pond. They may produce a light sprinkling of snow.

If long stripes of cloud drive at a slow rate, high in the air, and gradually become larger, the sky having been previously clear, expect rain.

When large masses gather simultaneously in the north-east and south-west, with the wind east, expect cold rain or snow within a few hours. The wind will back to the north.
(C.L. Prince)

NIMBO-STRATUS:

THE CLOUD OF LIGHT RAIN

Literally, 'rain layer'

Simply called 'nimbus', these are low, uniform, basic rain-cloud, 300-2000 feet. Thick enough to blot out the sun, they can disgorge continuous rain or snow.

Nimbo-status forms from alto-stratus which came too close to earth.

When scattered patches of nimbo-stratus come from the south-west, they are said by sailors to be 'prophet clouds' for they indicate wind.

If a little cloud appears in a clear sky, especially if it come from the west or somewhere in the south; there is a storm brewing.
(Bacon)

If there be long points, tails or feathers hanging from the thunder or rain clouds, five or six degrees above the horizon, with little wind in the summer, thunder may be expected but the storm will be of short duration.

STRATUS:

HILL CLOUD

Literally 'layer'

Resembling fog and often covering hills, stratus may bring drizzle. Harbingers of fine weather are when the day breaks out from the morning fog. Stratus at night is followed by a fine day if barometer stays high.

When mountains extend north and south, if fog or mist comes from the west, expect fair weather. If mist comes from the top of the mountains, expect rain in summer, snow in winter.
(Apache Indians)

Thin, white, fleecy broken mist, slowly ascending the sides of a mountain whose top is covered, predicts a fair day.
(Scotland)

When the clouds on the hilltops are thick and in motion, rain to the south-west is regarded as certain to follow.
(Scotland)

If mists rise to the hilltops and there stay, expect rain shortly.

Clouds upon hills, if rising, do not bring rain; if falling, rain follows.

When mist comes from the hill,
Then good weather it doth spill;
When mist comes from the sea,
Then good weather it will be.
(Kirkcudbright)

When mountains and hills appear capped by clouds that hang about and embrace them, storms are imminent.
(Bacon)

When Olympus, Athos, and generally all hills that give indications, have their tops clear, it indicates fair weather.
(Theophrastus)

In whatever direction a cloud stretches out from a mountain peak, in that direction will the wind blow.
(Theophrastus)

Whenever the clouds girdle the mountains quite down to the sea, it is a sign of fair weather.
(Theophrastus)

When the South Downs look blue and near after heavy rain, a gale may be expected within 36 hours.
(C.J Prince)

Banner cloud on the lee side of the Matterhorn, Switzerland. (Swiss National Tourist Office)

THE RISING OF THE MOON

When the moon is above the horizon, it attracts more atmosphere to itself and the atmosphere stretches, creating a larger area of air. The amount can be 25% between phases. If the useful atmosphere is 5 miles thick, then this stretch could be 1.25 miles, or for an accepted total depth of atmosphere of 60 miles, the atmospheric-tidal difference between high and low can be up to 15 miles. The result is a higher pressure than is the case where the moon is gone; at that time visiting the opposite hemisphere. As the moon rises, the clouds dissipate. Around a high pinnacle we may see a rising and lowering of a bank clouds, like a huge natural barometer, as the moon either rises or sets.

The higher the moon, the higher the clouds.
The higher the clouds, the finer the weather.

True cumulous clouds are more evident when the moon is out of the sky. They have crisp clean edges, as if shaped with a modelling knife. When the moon rises these edges become blurred and fuzzy because of the air-expansion aloft that accompanies the moon.

Soft-looking or delicate clouds foretell fine weather, with moderate or light breezes; hard-edged, oily looking clouds, wind.

The softer the clouds look the less wind (but perhaps the more rain) may be expected and the harder, more "greasy", rolled, tufted or ridged, the stronger the wind will prove.

If thick, resembling flocks, or rather great heaps of wool, be gathered in many places, they show rain. When thick dark clouds, right over the north or somewhat declining to the west, are close to the earth, rain immediately follows. If they appear like hills some way

from the earth, it is a sign of good weather. Black clouds signal rain, white clouds in winter on the horizon two or three days together indicate rain and snow.
(L. Digges, 1555)

While any of the clouds, except nimbo-stratus, retain their primitive forms, no rain can take place; and it is by watching changes and transitions that weather may be predicted.
(Howard)

SIGNS OF CHANGE

A sure sign of impending weather change is the condition known as "mares tails", the candy-floss look of streaky high cirrus. Expect a change within 36 hours. If it has been raining, it will clear, and if not, then rain is coming. Cirrus both precedes and follows a frontal trough or depression.

After fine clear weather, the first signs in the sky of a coming change are usually light streaks, curls, wisps, or mottled patches of white distant clouds, which increase and are followed by an overcasting of murky vapour that grows into cloudiness. The higher and more distant such clouds seem to be, the more gradual but general, will be the coming change.
(Fitzroy)

WITHOUT RAIN

Clouds without rain in summer indicate wind.
(Theophrastus)

SCRATCHY LOOK

If clouds look as if scratched by a hen,
Get ready to reef your topsails then.

MORNING AND EVENING

When the clouds of the morn to the west fly away,
You may conclude on a settled, fair day.
At sunset with a cloud so black,
A westerly wind you shall not lack.

STORM

When a heavy cloud comes up in the south-west and seems to settle back again, look out for a storm.

FRETTED AND SPOTTED

If the sky, from being clear, becomes fretted and spotted all over with bunches of clouds, rain will soon fall.
(Shepherd of Banbury)

When clouds are stationary and others accumulate by them, but the first remain still, it is a sign of a storm.
(Theophrastus)

It is not just cirrus that denotes weather change: any cloud pattern that is streaky, in rows, layers, or changing height will also foretell rain. Cumulus can gather into 'towers' which signify the approach of large rain dumps.

If the clouds appear to drive fast when there is no wind, expect wind from that quarter from which they are driven. But if they gather and collect together, on the sun's approach to that part, they will begin to disperse;

and then if they disperse towards the north, it prognosticates wind; if towards the south, rain.
(Bacon)

NORTHWEST

In the north-west, before daylight, if there are small black clouds like flocks of sheep; it's a sure and certain sign of rain.
(Wing, 1642)

If a layer of thin clouds drive up from the north-west, and under other clouds moving more to the south, expect fine weather.
(United States)

EAST

In the North Atlantic, if clouds appear during an easterly wind to the south-west, with their points turning to the north-east, it is a sign of a south-west wind in twenty-four hours.
(Kalm, Travels)

SOUTH

If clouds drive up high from the south, expect a thaw.

LOW

Clouds floating low, and casting shadows on the ground, are usually followed by rain.
(United States)

DIFFERENT DIRECTIONS

If two strata of clouds appear in dry hot weather to move in different directions, they indicate thunder and rain to follow.

DIFFERENT HEIGHTS

> *Clouds floating at different heights show different currents of air, and the upper one generally prevails. If this is north-east, fine weather may be expected; if south-west, rain.*
> (C.L. Prince)

If clouds float at different rates, directions and heights, expect heavy rains.

GUSTS

If there be a cloudy sky, with dark clouds driving fast under high clouds, expect violent gusts of wind.

RED

Red clouds at sunrise foretell wind; at sunset in the west, a fine day for the morrow.

Narrow, horizontal clouds after sunset indicate rain within thirty-six hours.

Red clouds in the east: rain the next day.

GREEN

Greenish tinted masses collecting in the south-east and remaining for several hours indicate heavy rains and gales. Green, especially at sunset, foretells rain.

BLACK

Dark clouds in the west at sunrise indicate rain on that day, clay-coloured and muddy clouds portend rain and wind. After black clouds; clear weather.

LIGHT

Delicate, quiet tints or colours, with soft, undefined forms of clouds, indicate and accompany fine weather; but unusual or gaudy hues, with hard, definitely outlined clouds, foretell rain, and probably strong wind.
(Fitzroy)

SCUD

Light scud-clouds driving across heavy masses show wind and rain, but if alone may indicate wind only
.(Fitzroy)

ROCKS AND TOWERS

When clouds appear like rocks and towers,
the earth's refreshed with frequent showers

INCREASING

A smallish, increasing white cloud about the size of a hand to windward is a sure precursor of a storm. A bench, or bank of clouds in the west means rain.
(Surrey)

MIST, FROST & FOG

A white mist in the evening, over a meadow with a river, will be drawn up by the sun the next morning, and the day will be bright.

MIST

White mist in winter indicates frost.
(Scotland)

QUICK

If mists rise in low ground and soon vanish, expect fair weather.
(Shepherd of Banbury)

HIGH

Where there are high hills, and the mist which hangs over the low lands draws towards the hills in the morning and rolls up to the top, it will be fair; but if the mist hangs upon the hills, and drags along the woods there will be rain.
(Rev W Jones)

DISPERSING

*Mists dispersing on the plain
Scatter away the clouds and rain;
But when they rise to the mountain-tops,
They'll soon descend in copious drops.
If the dew in evaporated immediately upon the sun rising, rain and storm follow in the afternoon; but if it stays and glitters for a long time after sunrise, the day continues fair.*
(De Quincey's "Note to Analects From Richter")

DEW

EVENING

If the dew lies plentifully on the grass after a fair day, it is a sign of another. If not, and there is no wind, rain must follow.
(Rev. W. Jones)

FINE WEATHER

Dew is an indication of fine weather; so is fog.
(Fitzroy)

CALM

Dew is produced in serene weather and in calm places.
(Aristotle)

HEAVY

If there is a heavy dew, it indicates fair weather; no dew, it indicates rain.

RAIN

If nights three dewless there be
T'will rain, you're sure to see.

FOG

If it's foggy in the morning, then it'll be a sunny day.
A foggy morning with dew on the grass indicates a clear day.
When the fog falls, fair weather follows; when it rises, rain ensues.
If fog forms on water in the fall or spring, a frost is on the way.
If there be a damp fog or mist, accompanied by wind, expect rain.
Five or six fogs successively drawn up portend rain.
Fog goes a hoppin', rain comes a droppin'
(USA)

FROST

RIVER

In the evenings of autumn and spring, vapour arising from a river is regarded as a sure indication of coming frost.
(Scotland)

Bearded frost
Forerunner of snow.
If frost melts before the sun rises, rain will follow.
A heavy white frost in winter is followed by a thaw.
(United States)

*A single white frost is often the sign of a fine day.
Three white frosts then a storm..*
(E.J. Lowe)

So far as the frost penetrates the earth in winter, so far will heat in summer.
(Systema Agriculturie J.W. 1681)

In winter, when the sky at midday has a greenish appearance to the east or northeast, snow and frost are expected.
(Scotland)

If there be a dark grey sky with a south wind, expect frost.

The surest indication of good weather is when the heavens seems further away from us than usual.
(Prof. Boerne's Latin MS,. 1677 to 1799)

In winter months, a clear moon means frost is on the way.

EARTHQUAKES

Earthquakes mostly occur when the perigeal or apogeal moon is at either declination (stitial colure) or crossing the equator (lunar equinox), and within one or two days of either of these. A detailed glance at any earthquake gathering station will reveal that around these dates the numbers of quakes rise steeply and then drop-off afterwards as the moon moves out of those declination zones. Close perigee and full Moon or new moon adds to the potential for increased earthquake activity along the moon's path between the latitudes.

As to time of day, earthquakes occur mostly when the atmospheric tide is at its lowest that day, at moonrise or moonset, or at IC point. If at new or full moon that means in early morning, late afternoon/evening or around midday.

Surges of activity come just after maximum northern declination for 4 days, then just after maximum southern declination for 3 days, globally. Earthquakes producing compressive north/south oriented faults tend to occur around maximum lunar declination in the *other* hemisphere, with rifting areas/expansive faults in the *same* hemisphere. East/West oriented faults like in Turkey tend to concentrate around the lunar equator crossings.

A stillness is often reported just prior to an earthquake, and on a day with no wind and high pressure. It is possible that the high pressure itself is a final trigger, helping to further depress the tectonic plates. There is little doubt left of the moon's role. When Apollo 11 left seismic equipment on the moon, it was observed to shake every time Earth came near. Logically the same phenomenon occurs on Earth whenever the moon draws near.

The first precise description of animal behaviour before an earthquake dates from 373BC and concerns the city of Helice in Achaia, the region of Greece bordering the Gulf of Corinth. Helice was destroyed that year by an especially violent earthquake, sank into the ground in the course of geological upheavals, and was swallowed forever by the sea. Five days before this thriving city sank from sight, reports the Greek historian Didorus (Didorus Siculusfl, 1st century BC) all animals that had been in it, such as rats, snakes, weasels, centipedes, worms, and beetles, migrated in droves along the connecting road toward the city of Koria, and the inhabitants of Helice were said to have been much puzzled. Pliny the Elder was a Roman writer and scientist who, at the eruption of Vesuvius in 79AD paid for his curiosity with his life. In his Natural History he wrote "even the birds do not remain sitting fearlessly." As early as 469BC a rabbit was mentioned as having had 'a premonition in connection with an earthquake in Sparta. Geese were kept at the Capitol in Ancient Rome to announce approaching danger with their honking. Just prior to the 1783 earthquake in Calabria, the howling of the dogs in the streets of Messina was so loud that an order was issued to kill them.

It is the shaking that presumably is picked up by animals close to ground, especially those with paws.

All the dogs left town before the buildings crashed down.
(Fitzroy, on the Galcahuasco Earthquake of 1855)

The Tibetan yak sprawls on the ground. The panda holds his head and screams. The swan gets up from the water and lays on the ground. Then we know an earthquake is coming.
(China)

We noticed how rats would flee into the open just before a cave-in.
(German miner, 1892)

THUNDER, LIGHTNING, HAIL & CYCLONES

Electrical storms are more common when the moon is out of the sky, which can mean overnight on a new moon or daytime over full moon. The lunar equinox(moon crossing equator) sees more thunderstorms than at any other declination, and the Last Quarter moon-to-New moon is the most common phase for them to occur.

In the Austrian Tyrol, the practice of ringing church bells had two functions. How far the sound reached was of interest to villagers. If they could hear it too clearly from afar, it was thought that bad weather was approaching. There may be much truth in this: a compacted atmosphere allows sound to travel further.

> *The ringing of bells is heard at a greater distance before rain; but before wind it is heard more unequally, the sound coming and going, as we hear it when the wind is blowing perceptibly.*
> (Bacon)

But it was also thought that the sound itself could dissipate thunder and lightning. This practice survived into the twentieth century.

THUNDER ON NEW MOON

When it thunders on the day of the moon's disappearance (new moon) the crops will prosper and the market will be steady.
(Assyrian Cuneiform records, 7th century BC)

CONTINUOUS

When the thunder is more continuous than lightning, there will be great winds; but if it lightens frequently between the thunderclaps, there will be heavy showers with large drops.
(Bacon)

FIRST THUNDER

After the first thunder comes the rain.
(Zuni Indians)

Thunder in the Fall foretells a cold Winter.

HEAT AND THUNDER

Great heats after the summer solstice generally end in thunderstorms; but if these do not come, in wind and rain. which last for many days.
(Bacon)

Thunder and lightning early in winter or late in autumn indicate warm weather

MORNING

Morning thunders signify wind; noon thunders, rain; roaring thunders, rough wind; crackling acute thunders,

wind and rain.
(Systema Agriculture, J.W. 1681)

When it thunders in the morning, it will rain before tonight.

Thunder in the morning denotes winds; at noon, showers.
(Bacon)

Morning thunders signify wind;
noon thunders, rain;
roaring thunders, rough wind;
crackling acute thunders, wind and rain.
(Systema Agriculturie, J.W.1681)

A winter thunderstorm was once thought to be an omen of death for a great man. Thunder in spring rain will bring. Thunder in the evening often means several days of wet, sultry weather.

WHERE THUNDER AND LIGHTNING COMES FROM

Lightning heats up the air along its path to around 30,000 degrees Celsius, causing the air to expand explosively and generating a shock wave that becomes a booming sound wave which is thunder. There is a sudden collapse of the cylinder of air heated by a lightning stroke. The electricity of the lightning initially heats the air to white heat, but then there is an equally sudden cooling caused by the loss of the energy radiating away in the flash. The air expands in the heating and then shrinks in the cooling, so the cylinder implodes. As light travels so fast, we see the lightning flash an instant after it occurs, but the noise of thunder is much slower, about 330 metres per second, so it takes

about 3 seconds to travel a kilometre. We can work out how far away the lightning strike was. If you see lightning and count to nine before you hear the thunder, the lightning would have occurred about 3 kilometres away. Thunder can usually be heard up to about 15 kilometres from the lightning discharge, but rarely at points more than 25 kilometres away. So sometimes you can see the lightning, but are too far away to hear the thunder. Lightning generally occurs with cumulonimbus clouds, particularly those in which hail is forming, as these tend to generate the areas of electrical charge, that are necessary for the formation of lightning, and hence thunder.
(courtesy Project Atmosphere, Australia)

If the lightning is in the colder quarters of the heaven, as the north and north-east, hailstorms will follow; but if in the warmer, as the south and west, there will be showers with a sultry temperature.
(Bacon, 1605)

Lightning in the north will be followed by rain in twenty-four hours.
(Spanish)

An old rhyme speaks of which tree is least likely to attract a lightning strike, and therefore should be sheltered under if caught outside during a storm:

*'Beware of the oak, it draws the stroke,
Avoid the ash, it courts the flash,
Creep under a thorn, it will save you from harm'.*

IN MYTHOLOGY

Storms were often considered to be an omen of divine wrath, and in most ancient cultures a person struck and killed by lightning was thought to have been directly struck down by a deity. In ancient Rome, a person killed this way was hastily buried without extensive mourning rites, and it was also frowned upon to rebuild any home struck by lightning.

In Britain in past centuries, a storm was usually considered the work of the devil; witches were also often accused of raising storms and at witch trials accusations were often made of deliberate attempts to damage property or sink ships by raising a storm. Black cats, considered agents of the Devil and which were believed to change into witches and back again at will, were carried on ships as insurance against the possibility of storms. If kept on land, the black cat was shut in the cupboard until the ship had sailed.

Some people still cover all the mirrors in their house during a thunderstorm; as it used to also be believed that windows and doors should be left open so that if the thunder got into the house, it could get out without having to damage anything.

HAIL

Hail brings frost in the tail;
Hail is rare in winter (Aristotle)
A hailstorm by day denotes a frost at night.
The sky turns green in a storm when there is hail.

CYCLONES

Cyclones, called typhoons in the East and hurricanes in North America, develop only when the seas reach a temperature of about 28 degrees Celsius and this usually occurs when the sun is over a particular hemisphere and close to or past its solstice position of that tropic, which will allow sufficient time for the sun's rays to heat the sea to that critical temperature.

The reason there are no cyclones off Brazil is probably due to the very large volume of cold fresh water from the Amazon that keeps the temperature of the adjacent oceans below that required for a cyclone to form.

Where conditions are warm enough for them to form, the heating process will continue after the moon has crossed the equator and into the other hemisphere. The build-up of heat will be speeded to that level during a Full Moon phase and into the Last Quarter because that is the time for the low atmospheric tide, both from the moon being a night moon and because the moon is over the opposite hemisphere. Cyclones mainly form around this time, on either side of and more than 5 degrees from the equator, but they never cross the equator.

Also, if the moon is at perigee, the atmospheric tide will be even lower because of the greater gravitation effect from the moon in that period.

Tropical cyclones generally move, as a whole, to the westward, curving to the north in northern latitudes (and to the south in southern latitudes). British cyclones generally travel in a north-east direction.

In the northern hemisphere, the circulation of air around cyclones is from east to west by way of north, or anticlockwise, which is against the course of the sun. Anticyclones, or fine weather see wind circling in the opposite direction, clockwise, the same course as the sun. Wind usually changes from east to west by way of south, or clockwise. In the southern hemisphere everything is reversed.

When the winds get to 34 knots (63 kilometres per hour) the low pressure system gets to be called a tropical cyclone or tropical storm. When the winds get to 63 knots (117 kilometres per hour) it is called a typhoon in the north-west Pacific Ocean. The dangerous part of the cyclone season in either hemisphere is mainly between the summer solstice and the next equinox. Stone circles were used as calendar markers.

If swans fly toward the wind, it is certain indication of a hurricane within 24 hours.

Painting by Gainor Jackson

TORNADOES, CLOUDBURSTS & WATERSPOUTS

Tornadoes usually form in the trailing edge of a thunderstorm. Wind speeds can reach 300 mph. Conventional radar cannot see a tornado... it only sees the rain, and hail.

Tornadoes generally move toward the north-east at 25 to 35 mph when associated with fronts, and squall lines but can travel at 70 mph. The first gust of wind to reach you from a thunderstorm is frequently the strongest. Wall clouds form on the rain free base often 15 to 20 minutes before the tornado occurs. Most wind damage is done by straight-line winds, not by tornadoes. With straight-line wind damage, all the damage will look like it diverges (moves outwards) from a single point possibly in several directions. With tornado damage, destruction is generally along one direction, debris along the ground is twisted or has spiral characteristics, and often small arcs where the top-soil has been removed are visible.

Tornadoes will mostly only occur before the moon has risen or after it has set. A tornado at night is therefore during the new moon; in the early hours of the morning and up to midday - First Quarter. But most tornadoes occur when the moon is full and into the Last Quarter, for this is the time that the sun applies more heat to the ground. Cloudbursts and waterspouts occur most at this time, too, and for the same reasons.

Dogs eat grass. It almost always happens before we have a major outbreak of tornadoes.

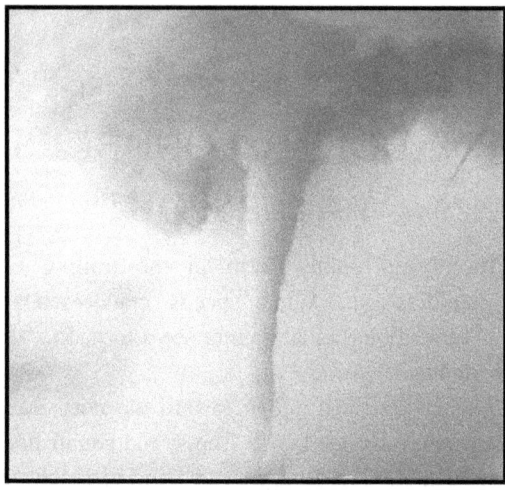

Waterspout over the sea

SEA, SURF & HILLS

It is said that in Auckland, you could once hear the Piha surf from New Lynn. That is about 40 miles away, and those halcyon days devoid of built up housing and traffic noise are gone. The author lived right beside the pounding of the East Coast sea for nearly ten years. Those who still live beside it know that when the sea sounds loud, a storm is approaching. The answer may lie in the wind, carried in by the sea by friction of the surface of the water. The same is said about the rustling in the trees, by dwellers on the outskirts of forests.

CALLING OF THE SEA

A murmuring or roaring noise, sometimes heard several miles inland during a calm, in the direction from which the wind is about to spring up, is known as the calling or the song of the sea.

FOREST AND MOUNTAIN

When the forest murmurs and mountain roars
Then close your windows and shut your doors.

FROM COAL

In the collieries about Dysart, and in some others, it is thought by the miners that before a storm of wind a sound not unlike that of a bagpipe or the buzz of the bee comes from the mineral, and that previous to a fall of rain the sound is more subdued.
(Sir Arthur Mitchell)

TRAIN WHISTLE

Sounds are heard with unusual clearness before a storm. The railway whistle, for instance, sees remarkably shrill.

TURN OF TIDE

Showers occur more frequently at the turn of the tide.

If, after the first ebb of the tide, it flows again for a little while, a storm approaches.
(Scottish coast)

WIND

The sea swelling silently and rising higher than usual in the harbour, or the tide coming in quicker than ordinary, prognosticates wind.
(Bacon)

EBB AND FLOW

If it raineth at tide's flow,
You may safely go and mow;
But if it raineth at the ebb,
Then, if you like, go off to bed.

SWELL

If, in the absence of wind, the surface of the sea becomes agitated by a long rolling swell, a gale may be expected. This was well known to seamen.

SURF

On the west coast, a heavy surf is considered the forerunner of a storm; while on the east a peculiar ripple, called a *twine* along the surface is known to precede a gale from the southeast.

DIM

Before rain the sea appears dim.
(Systema Agriculturie, J.W.1681)

SIGH OF THE SEA

Just before a storm, the sea heaves and sighs.
(Fitzroy)

NOISY BUT CALM

When the surface of the sea in harbour appears calm, and yet there is a murmuring noise within it, although there is no swell, a wind is coming.
(Bacon)

SEA FOAM

When the foam retreats and goes out, it is said in Rosehearty to be looking for more rough weather.
(Walter Gregor, Folklore Journal)

FOAM IN RIVER

Much foam in a river foretells a storm.
(Scotland)

FOAM GLITTERING

Glittering foam (called sea-lungs) in a heavy sea, foretells that the storm will last many days.
(Bacon)

PHOSPHORESCENCE

When the phosphorescence of the sea is seen during a dark night on the break of a roll, or on the water as it breaks on the rocks, it is said to indicate coming foul weather.
(Folklore Journal)

SOUND OF WAVES

When waves break on shore with long, hollow, rolling billows, bad weather is approaching.

SMOKE RISING

Smoke rising straight into the air means fair weather and smoke hanging low means rain is on the way.

With the high pressure approaching and the air becoming stretched, smoke will rise whereas with low pressure it can't rise and tends to lay low.

Rainbows & Sky

A rainbow is really a high distant mist, shone upon by the sun at an appropriate refractive angle so as to disperse white light into its spectral colours. For a rainbow to form there must be clouds of a certain height, and this is most often possible with the moon out of the sky. It is unusual to see rainbows around midday, except in winter and also in more extreme latitudes, because the sun is usually not low enough at that time to strike the clouds sideways. The rainbow has had many meanings in many cultures, the main similarity being that it was always connected with deities. In the Christian Bible the rainbow was set in the sky as God's pledge that there would never again be a great flood. In Burma the rainbow is a dangerous spirit; in India it is a bow from which divine arrows are fired. In Norse mythology the rainbow is the bridge that Odin built from Midgard, the home of men, to Asgard where the gods lived, and the souls of the worthy dead passed along the rainbow. In ancient Rome the rainbow was the many-coloured robe of Isis, attendant to Juno.

It was lucky to see a rainbow, and to wish when it was first seen, but unlucky to point directly at it, which would lead to bad luck or at least to the return of the rain. In Ireland, anyone who found the place where the rainbow touches the ground would supposedly find a pot of gold at its foot - most children know this story even today and imagine themselves doing it.

TIME OF THE DAY

If seen in the morning, a rainbow is always in the west and in the evening, in the east. Rainbow in the west means rain is coming, rainbow in east means the rain is going.

A rainbow at noon portends a heavy shower soon.

Rainbow in the eastern sky, the morrow will be dry.

Rainbow in the west that gleams, rain falls in streams.

Small broken pieces of rainbow appearing on a cloudy sky are sometimes called Weather-galls, and signify storms and blustery weather.

If a rainbow fades very quickly, good weather is on the way.

HEIGHT AND DISTANCE

When the rainbow does not reach down to the water, clear weather will follow. A rainbow low down on the mountains is said to be a bad sign for the crops.

If a rainbow be seen at a great distance, expect fair weather.

COLOURS

Red means wind, green means rain and blue means clearing. If red be the strongest colour there will be rain and wind together. If blue predominates, weather is clearing.

When a perfect rainbow shows only two principal colours, which are generally red and yellow, expect fair weather for several days. If green is large and bright it is a sign of continued rain.

When the rainbow is broad, with the prismatic colours very

distinct, and green or blue predominating, expect much rain the following night. If the red colour is the last to disappear, expect rain and wind.

The peasants of Anaphi could foretell the crops by the colours of the rainbows. If red prevailed, the crop would be abundant; if green, that of olives; if yellow, that of corn.

LONGER RANGE

Rainbow in spring generally means fair weather for 24 hours.

After much wet weather the rainbow is a sign of clearing up.

If the rainbow disappears all at once, there will follow serene and settled weather.

The appearance of double or triple bows indicates fair weather for the present, but heavy rains soon.

A rainbow in the morning denoted luck, in the evening, woe.

After a long drought, the rainbow is the precursor of a decided change to wet weather; a perfect bow, after an unsettled time, is a precursor of fair weather.

STARS

In many traditions and cultures stars are thought to be the souls of either unborn souls, or those who had passed away. In some cultures a shooting star foretells a birth, and is said to be the soul racing to animate the newborn baby, while in other places the shooting star foretells a death, or a soul released from purgatory. In some Native American traditions the Milky Way was considered a soul-road, where souls travelled on their journey after death, and that the brightest stars were campfires by which they rested on their travels.

It is unlucky to point at a star, or to try to count them. However, making a wish on the first star of evening will ensure its fulfilment, especially if the wisher repeats the old rhyme:

Star light, star bright
First star I see tonight
Wish I may, wish I might
Have the wish I wish tonight.

The wish made while a shooting star is seen in the sky would only be granted if made very quickly.

An old French cure for pimples was to pass a cloth over them while a shooting star fell.

Cold is the night, when stars shine bright.

OBSCURING

The obscuring of smaller stars in a clear night is a sign of rain.
(Wing, Ephemeris, 1649)

High cirrus clouds are not visible at night, but may conceal some stars.

TWINKLING

If the stars look larger and brighter than usual, and very flickery, rain or a storm may be on the way.

Twinkling means weather is about to change.

Excessive twinkling indicates heavy dews, rain, snow or stormy weather to come.

This is because far-off stars twinkle, whilst the nearer planets do not. The light from the more distant sources is weaker, and more subject to disruption from solar energy, which can adversely affect Earth's weather.

DISAPPEARED

If faint stars have disappeared and cannot be seen at all, the wind is about to rise

MANY STARS

When the sky seems very full of stars expect rain, or, in winter, frost.

When the air is very clear and the stars bright, with the moon absent, it is probably a New moon phase or First Quarter. Because the moon is absent, the glare from its light does not interfere with the view of the stars. The New moon time brings potential for rain or extra cool temperatures because of the extra gravitational pull of both new moon and sun acting together. The air-tide is deeper, and when lower, due to the moon being on the opposite side of the earth and leaving a depleted atmosphere above the horizon, the cold of space can more easily descend towards earth. A New moon means a day moon, when the moon is in the sky after sunrise. The rain will tend to be less when the moon is above the horizon, especially in winter.

If all stars are out at night
it will be a nice day tomorrow.

SIRIUS

If it does not rain at the rising of Sirius or Arcturus, there will generally be rain or wind about the equinox.

PLEIADES

> *If the Pleiades rise fine they set rainy, and if they rise wet they set fine.*
> (Swahili Proverb)

> *Rains and showers follow upon the rising of the Pleiades and Hyades, but without wind; storms upon the rising of Orion and Arcturus.*
> (Bacon)

HALOS

RINGS AROUND MOON

When the moon is in her house, rain or snow will come.

A ring around the moon brings rain or snow. Another similar saying is:

When the Moon is circled by a misty ring, it means rain to come. If the circle is large, it will rain very soon. Several concentric circles means a long period of wet weather.

When the moon has a halo or ring around it, this is due to cirrus clouds in the higher altitudes. Cirrus and cirrostratus clouds typically proceed low pressure systems bearing moisture. These clouds also contain ice crystals which refract the light giving the impression of a ring. By counting the number of stars contained within the ring, you can fairly accurately predict how far away the rain or snow will be. Each star represents approximately 24 hours of time (a faint star gets 12).

Ring near, water far;
Ring far, water near.
(Italy)

Haloes round the moon, a blood red sunset, a red moon
on her fourth rising prognostics of wind.
(Bacon)

The open side of the halo tells the quarter from which the wind or rain may be expected.

A halo round the moon is a sign of wind.
(China)

For I fear a hurricane
Last night the moon had a golden ring
And tonight no moon we see.
(Longfellow, Wreck of the Hesperus)

If the moon shows a silver shield
Be not afraid to reap your field;
But if she rises haloed round
Soon we'll tread on deluged ground.

MOON COLORS

PALE

A pale moon indicates rain; a red moon indicates wind.

DIM

When the moon has a white look, or when her outline is
not clear, rain or snow is looked for.
(Scotland)

YELLOW

A bright clear yellow moon rising in a cloudless sky means fine weather to come.

RED

> *If on her cheeks you see the maiden's blush,*
> *The ruddy moon foreshows that winds will rush*
> (Virgil)

> *The moon, her face if red be,*
> *Of water speaks she.*
> (Zuni Indians of the Southwest)

The red colour is due to the presence of dust being pushed ahead of a low pressure front bringing in moisture.

DARK MOON

When the moon is darkest near the horizon, expect rain.

SKY COLORS

> *A red morn, that ever yet betokened wreck to the seaman, tempest to the field, sorrow to shepherds, woe unto the birds, gust and four flaws the herdsmen and herds.*
> (Shakespeare)

Evening red and morning grey will set the traveller on his way; but evening grey and morning red will bring down rain upon his head.

A setting red sun means it'll be hot tomorrow.

If red the sun begin his race,
Be sure the rain will fall apace.

If red the sun set in grey
The next will be a rainy day.

A dark, gloomy blue sky is windy, but a light, bright blue sky indicates fine weather.

A bright yellow sky at sunset indicates wind; a pale yellow, wet.

WHY THE SKY IS BLUE

When light from the sun meets the billions of tiny gas or dust molecules in the atmosphere, the radiant energy is refracted or scattered in all directions. Because the molecules are so tiny, the shorter wave length light is scattered far better, so we get the blue of the sky. Late in the day when the sun is going down, sunlight has to travel longer distances through more atmosphere, and most of the light is scattered, except the reds.

Dust also causes rain to fall, because condensation nuclei are needed for the water molecules to condense. Dust is left behind after the water dries, which is why your car windscreen needs a clean after a rainfall.

SUN DOGS

A 'Sun Dog' is the equivalent of a halo around the moon. If the weather is foggy and you see a sun dog, expect the fog to clear shortly. Halos around the moon and sun dogs are both rainbows

If you look up around the middle of the day and see a rainbow or white band around the sun, look for a drastic change in the weather within 12 - 24 hours. If the weather is clear, plan on stormy weather and if the weather is dreary, plan on fair weather to arrive.

RED SUN

A red sun at dusk or dawn indicates dry weather. Compare this with a red sky at dusk or dawn as some people tend to confuse these two.

At dusk, a red sky indicates that dry weather is on the way. This is due to the sun shining through dust particles being pushed ahead of a high pressure system bringing in dry air. A red sky in the morning is due to the sun again shining through dust. In this case however, the dust is being pushed on out by an approaching low pressure system bringing in moisture.

Don't confuse a red sky in the morning with a red sun in the morning. If the sun itself is red and the sky is a normal colour, the day will be fair.

BAROMETER & CHANGES

A barometer is a tiny copy of the larger scene, as is a map of a landscape. Inside every instrument is a column of liquid; alcohol or mercury. Air pressure on the surface pushes the surface level down and that amount is simply measured against a scale etched alongside. The assumption is that this little micro-picture reflects what is happening on a grander scale at that geographical point. On the bigger scale millibars are the units of pressure of the weight of all the air in a supposed narrow column going right up to the top of the atmosphere above any fixed ground point.

The barometer was invented in 1645 as a three foot (900mm) glass tube. The aneroid barometer was invented in 1844. For many years these instruments remained the province of the scientists.

Because the barometer is adjusted to read at sea-level so that comparisons between locations can be made, there is no way to detect changing height of the atmosphere. To standardise pressure observations, meteorologists adjust the daily pressure observations to remove the effect of the atmospheric tide due to the moon. This is because the atmospheric tide varies and is not apparent in latitudes greater than 50-60 degrees, as the moon itself does not exceed 29 degrees in its declination range. By factoring out the moon in every computer weather model, the fact that the barometer has lasted unchanged until this day is remarkable, considering its limited inaccuracy. For instance, sometimes the barometric needle stays still while the weather can change. The needle may climb to around 1040mb in the middle of a downpour, when rain mostly kicks in only when under 1016mb.

Boyles Law states that pressure, volume and temperature in a fixed container all act dependently upon each other. We can think of the atmosphere, too, as a gas in a fixed container, kept intact by gravity and centrifugal force. Scientists and barometer salesmen inform us that the pressure change of the barometer indicates weather change, but volume and temperature fail to get any mention. Pressure, as when we put our finger against the table top, is when something is pushed. But the moon as a gravitational force cannot push anything. Gravitational force pulls, which is not quite the same thing.

One can liken it to sea-tides. Measuring the pressure of the waves coming up the beach with one's hand in the water will not tell if it is high or low tide. But volume of water at that point will. Volume *can* exert a pressure, but it need not do so. The barometer measures pressure, whereas what we want to establish, atmospherically-speaking, is volume. We want to know how much atmosphere is in a particular space, because more or less atmosphere, stretched or compacted, means more of Earth's protection against the two potential dangers to our environment: the searing heat of the sun and the freezing cold of space.

There is less atmosphere at the poles than at the equator, because the sun and moon are at the side of the earth and create a bulged atmosphere that is stretched higher at the equator. The difference is great, from 13 miles up in the mid-latitudes to only 1-2 miles up at the poles, where that protection is absent and the cold of space comes almost to ground level, freezing everything in sight. That is why Antarctica is covered with ice and snow all year around and why the ice at the poles will never melt. Sound can travel for a kilometre at the South Pole in the compacted air.

The best way to use the barometer to read weather changes is in conjunction with a thermometer. If the barometer stays the same but the temperature drops, there is a chance of rain. If the barometer stays the same but the thermometer rises, expect a clearing. If the barometer goes up but the thermometer stays the same, rain could ensue again. If the barometer rises or falls while the thermometer plunges, a thunderstorm could be close by. Barometer falling with thermometer rising: heavy rain. When both rise, either the wind is about to change or the weather is to improve; when both fall, weather is deteriorating quickly. So if the barometer is constant, it means rain or clearing; if it drops; rain, frost, or thaw, and if it rises; wind change, gale, rain, frost or clearing. The mercury level seldom falls for snow. A first rise after a low or a rapid rise can indicate unsettled weather.

The average rate of fall of the barometer when signalling a warm front(which can cause a depression, as does a cold front) is 2.5 mb/hr. For the first 5 hours the rate will be low(1 mb/hr), but over the next 5-10 hours the rate of fall increases. In about 4 hours the rate may be 3 mbs/hr – a gale warning.

No discussion about the history of barometers can be complete without mention of Robert Fitzroy, captain of the Beagle on which Charles Darwin sailed around the world in January 1832, The Beagle was heavily instrumented for the voyage, including several chronometers. The ship also carried barometers, which Fitzroy used it to good effect in short term weather forecasting. It was the first voyage with sailing orders that wind observations should be taken using the Beaufort wind scale.

Fitzroy served as a Member of Parliament for Durham in

1841, and Governor General of New Zealand. In 1854 he was appointed to head a new department that became the British Meteorological Office. Its initial mandate was to compile statistics on wind to assist the efficiency of navigation. He enlarged on that role promoting weather observations, establishing barometer stations, telegraphic reporting and, in 1861, the first storm warnings. These he soon extended to routine weather forecasts. It was he who introduced the first daily weather forecasts published in The Times in 1860.

Fitzroy advocated placing a barometer at every port so that seamen could read them before embarking on their journeys. In 1862 he published "The Weather Book" In the eyes of his conservative peers, the prediction techniques used were not up to the standard needed to establish credibility.

Also, he could not decide whether or not he was a "lunarist", having written conflicting opinions in his Weather Book, p3

> *"...solar heating is sufficient to ascribe all our atmospheric conditions and changes without at present drawing in any powerful lunar influence..."*

and on p4;

> *"...that the moon, as well as, and probably much more, than the sun, causes a tidal effect in air, due to gravitation, cannot be doubted..."*

and then again on p244

> *"...the moon acts on every particle of air, as on water and earth by universal gravitation. Tidal effects must therefore be caused by the moon and by the sun in earth's atmosphere, and their scales may be large in proportion to its depth and extreme mobility..."*

He was criticized in Parliament, newspapers and by other scientists, including Matthew Maury. His role in assisting Darwin also greatly troubled him; he had a conflict with his conscience and his religious beliefs. On April 30th 1865 he took his life by slashing his wrists at his home at Upper Norwood, outside London. The inquest respectfully attributed his action to overwork.

That his contribution was significant is not doubted. However, by refusing to be consistent in lunar theory (probably to satisfy his critics) he may have held up meteorology as a science for over 150 years, with an ongoing legacy to this day.

Fitzroy formulated 'forecasting remarks' that became popular and were inscribed on barometers. His table of helpful hints is printed on the next page.

BAROMETRIC CHANGES

- A fall of half a tenth of an inch or more in half an hour is a sign of storm.
- A fall when the thermometer is low indicates snow or rain.
- A fall with a rising thermometer indicates wind and rain from the southward.
- Sharp rise after low foretells stronger blow.
- Sinks lowest of all for the great winds, not necessarily with rain.
- Greatest heights are for easterly or north-easterly winds.
- In calm frosty weather, the mercury stands uncommonly high.
- After very great storms, it rises very fast.
- The more northerly places have greater alterations. In very hot weather, the falling indicates thunder. In winter, the rising presages frost, and in frosty weather, but if the mercury falls 3 or 4 divisions, there will be a thaw.
- If a continued frost and the mercury rises, there will be snow.
- Unsettled motion of mercury, uncertain changeable weather.
- Sudden fall in spring, winter or autumn means high winds and storms, but in summer heavy showers and thunder.
- When there has been no storm before or after the vernal equinox (March 21), the ensuing summer is dry, five times in six.
- Steady rise shows that fine weather may be expected, but in winter - frost.
- When rising: In winter the rise of the barometer presages frost.
- In wet weather if the mercury rises high and remains so, expect continued fine weather in a day or two.
- In wet weather if the mercury rises suddenly very high, fine weather will not last long.

- Fitzroy

BAROMETER RISING	
28.8 to 29.2 in.	Clearing, high winds and cool.
29.2 to 29.6 in.	High winds, cool, preceded by squalls.
29.6 to 29.9 in.	Fair, fresh winds next 24 hours.
29.9 to 30.2 in.	Fair, and brisk winds, diminishing.
30.2 to 30.5 in.	Fair weather, cooler, variable winds.
30.5 to 30.8 in.	Continued cool, clear, light winds.
30.8 to 31.0 in.	High winds, southeast with rain.

BAROMETER FALLING	
30.8 to 30.5 in.	Fair, warmer, followed by rain and wind.
30.5 to 30.2 in.	Approaching storm.
30.2 to 29.9 in.	Cloudy, warmer, unsettled.
29.9 to 29.6 in.	Unsettled, warmer with increasing wind.
29.6 to 29.3 in.	Squally, clearing, fair and cooler.
29.3 to 29.0 in.	Clearing, high winds, squalls and cooler.
29.0 to 28.7 in.	Stormy weather.

SIGNS

(Courtesy of N. Fares)

SIGNS OF DETERIORATING WEATHER:

- *Air smells clean and fresh.*
- *Cloud ceiling lowers.*
- *Puffy clouds begin to develop vertically and darken.*
- *Sky is dark and threatening to the west.*
- *Clouds increasing in numbers, moving rapidly across the sky.*
- *Clouds at different heights moving in different directions.*
- *Clouds moving from east or northeast towards the South.*
- *Heavy rain occurring at night.*
- *Barometer falling steadily or rapidly.*
- *Smoke from stacks lowers.*
- *Static on AM radio.*
- *Wind shifting north to east and possibly through east to south.*
- *There is a ring (halo) around the moon.*
- *If on land, leaves that grow according to prevailing winds turn over and show their backs.*
- *Strong wind and /or a red sky in the morning.*
- *Temperatures far above or below normal for the time of year.*
- *Small clouds join and thicken.*
- *Crickets and frogs are louder.*

SIGNS OF IMPENDING STRONG WINDS:

- *Light, scattered clouds alone in a clear sky.*
- *Sharp, clearly defined edges to clouds.*
- *Yellow sunset.*
- *Unusually bright stars.*
- *Major changes in the temperature.*

SIGNS OF IMPENDING PRECIPITATION:

- *Distant objects seem to stand above the horizon.*
- *Sounds are very clear and can be heard for great distances.*
- *Transparent veil-like cirrus clouds thicken, ceiling lowers.*
- *Hazy and sticky air. Rain may occur in 18-36 hours.*
- *Halo around the sun or moon.*
- *Increasing south wind with clouds moving from the West.*
- *Wind (especially north wind) shifting to west and then south.*
- *Steadily falling barometer.*
- *Pale sunset.*
- *Red sky to the west at dawn.*
- *No dew after a hot day.*

SIGNS OF CLEARING WEATHER:

- *Cloud bases rise.*
- *Smoke from stacks rise.*
- *Wind shifts to west, especially from east through south.*
- *Barometer rises quickly.*
- *A cold front has passed in the past 4 to 7 hours.*
- *Gray early morning sky shows signs of clearing.*
- *Morning fog or dew.*
- *Rain stopping and clouds breaking away at sunset.*

SIGNS OF CONTINUING FAIR WEATHER:

- *Early morning fog that clears.*
- *Gentle wind from the west or northwest.*
- *Barometer steady or rising slightly.*
- *Red sky to east with clear sky to the west at sunset.*
- *Bright moon and light breeze at night.*

- *Heavy dew or frost.*
- *Clear blue morning sky to west.*
- *Clouds dot the afternoon summer sky.*

IT WILL BE A COLD, SNOWY WINTER IF:

- *Squirrels accumulate huge stores of nuts*
- *Beavers build heavier lodges than usual.*
- *Hair on bears and horses is thick early in season.*
- *the breastbone of a fresh-cooked turkey is dark purple.*
- *crops of acorns are large.*

A severe summer denotes a windy autumn;
A windy winter denotes a rainy spring;
A rainy spring denotes a severe summer;
A severe summer denotes a windy autumn;

A month that comes in good, goes out bad.
A warm Christmas; a cold Easter.

YOUR NOSE AS A BAROMETER

If you find yourself out in a marsh or swamp and the air really seems to stink more than normal, expect rainy weather. This happens when the pressure drops and the methane trapped on the bottom of the swamp is released in greater quantities. In reverse, as fair weather approaches and the pressure rises, things won't smell quite so strong.

YOUR EYES AS BAROMETER

Mountains and other far away objects will appears to be much closer and more sharply focused as wet weather approaches and the air pressure drops. The dust particles in the air begin to settle to the ground and the air clears allowing you to see more details of faraway objects. As a high pressure front approaches and the air becomes thicker, more dust particles become suspended in air and things take on their normal somewhat hazy appearance.

YOUR EARS AS BAROMETER

Sound too becomes sharper and more focused prior to stormy weather. Instead of traveling upward and outward into the atmosphere they are bent back to the earth and their range extended. Birds' calls sound sharper and you may hear the blowing of a train horn as it rumbles through a valley far away.

RISE AND FALL

When the glass falls low
Prepare for a blow;
When it slowly rises high,
Lofty canvas you may fly.

Quick rise arter low
Indicates a stronger blow;
Long foretold, long last,
Short notice, soon past

At sea with low and falling glass
Soundly sleeps a careless ass,
Only when it's high and rising
Truly rests a careful wise one.

ANIMALS, BIRDS, INSECTS & FISH

It is said that animals, birds, insects, fish and plants somehow 'know' when weather is going to be fair, stormy or otherwise calamitous. The same claims are sometimes made about pets being psychic. Tabloid stories abound of long forgotten cats and dogs making their way home again across several continents. Rather than possessing inner psychic powers, it is more probable that they are very sensitive to their environments. It is now known that the ends of a cat's whiskers can detect subtle and minute changes in air pressure. A mouse moving behind a hole will move the air in a room sufficiently to alert the cat. If true, then a cat will also be able to detect weather change, which is also an air pressure difference. If cats can do it then presumably so can other animals, and so presumably, can humans at some level.

SIGNS OF FINE WEATHER

Cat's skin looks 'bright.'
Cattle remain on hilltops.
Oxen lie on their left sides.
Goats graze up the mountains.
Sheep feed uphill in the morning.

Bats appear early in evening.
Thrushes sing at sunset.
Owls hoot quietly.
Hawks fly high.

When spiders weave their webs by Noon,
fine weather is coming soon

SIGNS OF WIND

Cats scratch posts or walls.
Cat licks herself with her face turned to the north wind
Cats or dogs put tails up and hair seems electrified.
Old sheep turn their backs towards the wind.
Pigs seem terrified.
Hawks fly low

SIGNS OF RAIN

Animals seek shelter
Animals crowd together
Dogs make holes in the ground
Dogs howl when people go out.
Dogs refuse meat.
Dogs eat grass.
Dogs roll on the ground and scratch, and become drowsy.
Spaniels sleep more than usual.
Cat sneezes.
Cat lies 'on its brain'
Cat stops frolicking.
Cats wipe their jaws with their feet, and their paws over their ears.
Horses stretch their necks and sniff the air.
Horses sweat in the stable.
Horses are restless and assemble in the corner of the field.
Young horses roll on the ground.

Wild ponies scamper and seek lower ground.
Donkeys prick ears forward and rub backs on walls.
Asses bray.
Cattle gaze at the sky, eat greedily and suddenly move here and there making noises.
Cows and sheep lie down.
Bulls kick about and lick hoofs.
Bulls lead going into pasture.
Oxen lick themselves against the hair.
Rams butt their heads.
Young sheep become frisky.
Old sheep huddle by trees and bushes.
Pigs carry straw to their pigsties.
Pigs' tails straighten.
Herons stand melancholy on the sand.
Birds return slowly to their nest
Birds peck themselves.
Birds roost early and feed heavily before rain or snow.
Redbirds or Bluebirds chatter.
Birds gather on a telephone wire.
Small birds duck and wash in the sand.
Fowls huddle together outside the hen-house.
Pigeons wash.
Parrots whistle.
Rooks fly low.
Snakes come out before rain.
The louder the frog, the more the rain.
Most reptiles become more agitated before a weather change.
Fishes in general, both in salt and fresh waters, sport most and bite more eagerly before rain than any other time.
If Ducks or Drakes their Wings do flutter high
Or tender Colts upon their Backs do lie,
If Sheep do bleat, or play, or skip about,
Or Swine hide Straw by bearing on their Snout,
If Oxen lick themselves against the Hair,

Or grazing Kine to feed apace appear,
If Cattle bellow, grazing from below,
Or if Dogs Entrails rumble to and fro,
If Doves or Pigeons in the Evening come
Later than usual to their Dove-House Home,
If Crows and Daws do oft themselves be-wet,
Or Ants and Pismires Home a-pace do get,
If in the dust Hens do their Pinions shake,
Or by their flocking a great Number make,
If Swallows fly upon the Water low,
Or Wood-Lice seem in Armies for to go,
If Flies or Gnats, or Fleas infest and bite,
Or sting more than they're wont by Day or Night,
If Toads hie Home, or Frogs do croak amain,
Or Peacocks cry
Soon after look for Rain!

SIGN FROM SEAGULL

Seagull, seagull sit on the sand.
It's never good weather when you're on the land.
Seabirds, stay out from the land,
We won't have good weather while you're on the sand.

SIGN FROM A COW

A cow with its tail to the West makes the weather best,
A cow with its tail to the East makes the weather least.

SIGNS FROM A CAT

Good weather may be expected when the cat washes herself, but bad weather may be expected when she licks her coat against the grain or washes her face over her ears, or sits with her tail to the fire.

SIGNS FROM A PIG

When pigs carry straw to their pigsties,
bad weather may be expected.

SIGN FROM SWALLOW (IN SUMMER)

Swallows high, staying dry;
Swallows low, wet will blow.

This relates to the feeding behaviour of swallows, their close relatives house martins, and other birds which feed on flying insects, such as swifts. On a fine summer's evening these birds will fly high in the sky, where the insects are gathering. This means that there is a high pressure system overhead, bringing fine weather for the days to come. Conversely, when swallows, martins and swifts fly low to catch insects, it is often windy and cloudy, the result of the imminent arrival of a depression, bringing bad weather. The 'tumbling' behaviour of rooks in autumn is also supposed to foretell a change in the weather: probably because this behaviour tends to occur during windy conditions, which usually signify the coming of a depression.

Other species of bird are often associated with rain, such as woodpeckers, whose habit of calling and drumming before the arrival of bad weather has given them the name 'rain bird' in many parts of Britain, Europe and North America. Another species, red-throated diver, is known in Shetland as the 'rain goose'. *(source: BBC Weather Centre)*

SIGN OF A SHOWER

Cow tries to scratch its ear.
Cow claps her tail against hedge.
Cows swirl tails, hold in air.

SIGNS OF THUNDER AND HAIL.

Cow thumps its ribs with its tail.
Birds fall silent.

SIGNS OF STORM

Unusual howling of dogs.
Wolves howl more.
Cows fail their milk.
Goats leave the high ground in search of shelter.
Goats graze down the mountains.
Old sheep eat greedily.
Old sheep leave the high ground and bleat much in the evening and during the night.
Hogs cry and run up and down with hay or litter in their mouths
Sheep and herds fight for their food more than usual.
Foxes, wolves, bats and mice utter shrill cries.
Birds fly in circles.
Sparrows chirp at dawn.
Seagulls alight in a field.
Horses run fast before a violent storm or before windy conditions.
Pigs gather leaves and straw.
Flowers close up
Rooster goes crowing to bed.
Ants are busy, gnats bite, crickets sing louder than usual, spiders come down from their webs, and flies gather in houses.
Cows will lie down and refuse to go out to pasture.
If the bull leads the cows to pasture, expect rain;
if the cows precede the bull, the weather will be uncertain.
The louder the frog, the more the rain.

Cranes soaring aloft and quietly in the air foreshows fair weather, but if they make much noise, as if consulting which way to go, if foreshadows a storm that's near at hand.

> *Hogs crying and running unquietly up and down with hay or utter in their mouths foreshadow a storm to be near at hand.*
> (Thomas Willsford)

SIGNS OF SNOW

Cats sit with their back to the fire.
Sheep bleat in a lower bass tone.
Hares take to the open country
Birds roost close to the ground.
Pigs and squirrels gather more debris to insulate themselves from cold weather.

SIGNS OF A THAW

Cats wash their faces.
Old sheep eat sparingly.
Hogs rub themselves.

SIGNS OF COLD

Horses and mules are very lively.
Sheep sniff the north breeze.
Migratory birds take flight too early.
Fowls stand on one leg.

SIGN OF A SEVERE WINTER

Cows lie on their right side.

SIGN OF A MILD WINTER

Cows lie on their left sides.

ROOSTERS

If cocks crow during a downpour, it will be fine before night.
If the rooster goes crowing to bed, he'll certainly rise with a watery head.

WATERLIFE

RISING

Fish rise to the surface and bite more before a storm.

JUMPING

Fish jump out of the water just before rain.
Fish bite the least
With wind to the east.

PORPOISES AND WHALES

When porpoises and whales spout about ships at sea, storms may be expected.
Porpoises swim into the wind.
Porpoises shelter in bays and round islands, before a storm.

DOLPHINS CHASING

> *Dolphins chasing one another foreshadow wind. If they play in rough weather, it indicates approaching calm.*
> (Thomas Willsford)

If they sport around a boat, it is considered unlucky and portending stormy weather.

SHARKS

Sharks go out to sea at the approach of cold weather.

UPSTREAM

Fish swim upstream before rain.

TROUT NOT BITING

When trout refuse a bait or fly
There ever is a storm a-nigh

EELS LIVELY

If eels are very lively, it is a sign of rain.

MULLET HEAD SOUTH

Mullet run south at the approach of cold northerly wind and rain.

COCKLES

> *Cockles, it is said, have more gravel sticking to their shells before a tempest.*
> (Thomas Willford)

AIR-BUBBLES

Air bubbles over clam beds indicate rain.

SEA ANEMONE

The sea anemone opens for rain, and closes for fine, clear weather.

LEECHES

Leeches remain on the bottom during fine weather, and calm wet weather. If a storm is approaching they move steadily upwards in an agitated fashion.

EARTHWORMS

If snails, worms or slugs appear, it presages rain.
Worms descend to a great depth either before a long drought or a severe frost.

SNAILS

When snails scale evergreens and remain there all day, expect rain.
(C.L. Prince)

GLOW-WORMS

When the glow-worm lights her lamp;
The air is always damp.
If glow-worms much shine,
T'will rain, two days' time.

INSECTS

EARLY APPEARANCE

The early appearance of insects indicates early spring and good crops.
(Apache Indians)

BEES

When many bees enter the hive and none leave it, rain is near.
(Scotland)

Bees early at work will not go on all day.

Bees won't swarm before a near storm. Swarming is then an indication of more fine weather.

Bees will go greater distances from home if the weather is fine, but stay close to hive if rain coming.

A bee was never caught in a shower.

ANTS

Ants withdraw into their nests, build walls, are more active and busy themselves with eggs before a storm.

When ants go for high ground it means there is going to be rain.

Expect stormy weather when ants travel in lines, and fair weather when they scatter.

If in the beginning of July the ants are enlarging their piles, an early and cold winter will follow.

An open ant-hole indicates clear weather; a closed one, an approaching storm.

Ants run faster or slower as the atmosphere gets hotter or colder.

WASPS

When wasps and hornets build their nests high on banks of a stream, expect a wet summer; but if low and near the surface of the water, a dry summer is indicated.
(C.L Prince)

If wasps build their nests high, the winter will be long and harsh.

Wasps in great numbers and busy indicate warmer weather.

SPIDERS

Spiders will spin thicker, bigger webs in when the weather is going to be dry.

Spiders work hard and spin their webs before the wind.
(Bacon)

If they make the lines long, the weather will be fine for fourteen days. If short, expect rain or wind.

If spiders are lazy, rain usually follows. Activity during rain indicates short duration.
(J.W.G. Gutch)

Spiders generally change webs once every twenty-four hours. If they make a change between 6pm and 7pm expect a fair night. If they change their webs in the morning, expect a fine day. Spiders seen crawling on walls more, indicate rain soon.

When they make their webs at high speed near the ground, expect rain.
(Ireland)

If they clean their webs, expect fine weather.

Long, single, separate spiders' webs on grass indicate frost next night.
(Ireland)

Funnel-shaped webs seen after drought mean change in weather within three days.
(C.L. Prince)

When spiders undo their webs, tempests follow.
If spiders fall from walls, it signifies rain.
Spiders in motion indicate rain.
Light cobwebs floating in lines along the air indicate rain soon.
Cobwebs on the grass are a sign of fair weather.

FLIES

Houseflies coming into the house indicate wind or rain.

BUTTERFLIES

The appearance of butterflies is said to indicate fine weather.

When the butterfly comes; comes also the summer.
(Zuni Indians)

When chrysalises are found suspended from railings and eaves, expect rain; but if from slender branches, fair weather.
(Western Pennsylvania)

GNATS

If gnats form a vertical column, expect fine weather.
If gnats fly in large numbers, the weather will be fine.

LOCUSTS

When locusts are heard, dry weather will follow, and frost will occur in six weeks.
(United States)

If cicadas' eggs lie head-upwards; a dry summer, if head downwards; a wet one.

CRICKETS

Crickets chirp faster as the temperature rises.
Crickets chirping loudly indicate a pleasant day to follow.
When crickets chirp unusually, expect wet weather.

CRICKET THERMOMETER

As they chirp quicker in warmer air, to determine air temperature (Fahrenheit), count the number of chirps in 14-seconds and add 40, or in 15 seconds and add 37.

FIRST CICADA

When you hear the first cicada of the summer, expect the first frost of the year in exactly 90 days.

WET SUMMER

Wood ducks are have greater numbers of chicks than normal.

PLANTS

In NZ there is a belief that when the cabbage tree blooms profusely, that there will be a long dry summer. If it flowers early, then that is another good omen. Another is the early flowering of flax. Yet no one has stated that ALL these blossom indications need to occur together before a supposed drier spell; or if only one tree or plant is sufficient to give a reading. A probable reason for profuse spring blooming is that the trees and plants, whichever and wherever they are, had a favourable autumn or winter.

Having said that, it does seem plants and certain fungi such as rainstars can accurately forecast the certainty of imminent wet and dry weather. Chickweed, dandelions, bindweeds, wild indigo, clovers, and tulips all fold their petals prior to the rain. Rainstars, a type of fungus, opens up prior to a rain and closes in dry weather. Mushrooms abound when the weather is moist as well as do mosses and seaweeds. In fact, seaweeds exposed on the rocks at low tide seem to swell and rejuvenate in the high humidity proceeding wet weather. When the atmosphere reaches about 80% humidity, the bog pimpernel closes and gives rise to this saying:

Pimpernel, pimpernel, tell me true
Whether the weather be fine or no;
No heart can think, no tongue can tell,
The virtues of the pimpernel.

DEAD BRANCHES

Dead branches falling in calm weather indicate rain.

BERRIES

Plenty of berries indicate a severe winter.

FLOWERS ODOUR

The odour of flowers is strongest just before a shower than at any other time.

BLOSSOMS

Early blossoms indicate a bad fruit year.

OAK AND ASH

> *If the oak before the ash comes out,*
> *There has been, or there will be, drought.*
> (Surrey)

> *The oak displaying many acorns foretells a long and hard winter.*
> (Worledge)

ROWAN TREE (MOUNTAIN ASH)

This is a tree in Finland whose name is "pihlaja" This tree has sort of pointed leaves and in the fall it has many berries in clusters. Pihlaja can't carry two heavy loads. This means that if there are many clusters of berries there won't be that much snow in the winter. The other interpretation is that many berries forecast a cold winter.

MAPLE

When the leaves of the sugar-maple turn upside down, expect rain.
(United States)

PINE-CONES

Pine-cones hung up in the house will open against hot and dry times, and close against wet and cold weather.
(Thomas Willsford)

NUTS

When there are plenty of nuts, expect a hot and dry harvest.
(C.L. Prince)

WHEAT

Abundant wheat-crops never follow a mild winter.
(C.W. Empson)

GOAT'S BEARD

Goat's Beard keeps its flowers closed in damp weather.
(C.L. Prince)

DANDELION

When the down on the dandelion leaf contracts, it is a sign of rain; sensitive plants contract their leaves with the approach of rain.

Dandelion blossoms close before a storm.

When dandelions bloom early in spring, it will be a short season.

When they bloom late, expect a dry summer.

RHODODENDRON THERMOMETER

Like the cricket, Rhododendrons have the unique ability to act as temperature gauges. As the air temperature rises, their leaves begin to unfurl. At 20 degrees they are completely closed and when the temperature reaches 60 degrees, they are completely open

CLOVER

Clover contracts its leaves at the approach of a storm.

DAISY

The daisy shuts its eye before rain.

OPEN ALL NIGHT

If flowers keep open all night, it will be wet the next day.

SEAWEED

A piece of sea weed, hemp or kelp hung up will become damp just before rain.

MUSHROOMS

The sudden growth of mushrooms presageth rain.
(Systema Agriculturie, J.W.1681)

When there are lots of berries on the dogberry tree, it means it's going to be a bad winter.
(USA)

LEAVES

If the leafs are turning up, a storm is brewing.
If autumn leaves are slow to fall, prepare for a cold winter.
When the leaves of trees turn over, it foretells windy conditions and possible severe weather

EXPECTED FLOWERING DATES (Northern Hemisphere)	
Hazel	January 9th
Coltsfoot	January 31st
Wood Anemone	March 2nd
Garlic Hedge Mustard	March 31st
Horse Chestnut	April 20th
Purple Lilac	April 22nd
Hawthorn	April 25th
Laburnum	April 27th
White Ox-Eye	May 5th
Elder	May 10th
Dog Rose	May 23rd
Greater Bindweed	June 13th
Harebell	June 21st
Madonna Lily	June 21st
Autumn Crocus	August 14th
Ivy	September 1st

PLANTING BY THE MOON

Go plant the bean when the moon s light,
and you will find that this is right;
plant the potatoes when the moon is dark,
and to this line you always hark,
but if you vary form this rule,
you will find you are a fool,
if you always follow this rule to the end,
you will always have money to spend.

If you plant by the dark of the moon, it makes more potatoes.
If you plant in the light of the moon, it makes more vine.

Crops that produce above the ground should be planted on days leading up to the full moon (waxing).
Root crops should be planted on days between the full moon and the new moon (waning)

If the temperature dips to 28 degrees when the moon is waning, fewer blooms are nipped and less fruit is lost.

The phases of the moon seems to be the fundamental element that most people agree upon. Fruit was always picked on full moon, when the colour was fullest and the fruit juiciest. The energy was considered to be at the extremities, where the fruit were. Sap, too, rises higher with full moon. Watering is mainly required at new moon time as the moon is rising with the sun in the morning, the double upward gravitational pull therefore draining the soil. Foods to be preserved and that were to last are picked more around new moon.

BUBBLES IN COFFEE

DREAMS

Dreams of hurrying or of frightful events, are frequent indications of wind(particularly easterly) or weather change.

ITCH

If corns, wounds or sores itch or ache more than usual, rain is to fall shortly.

RINGING IN EAR

A ringing or singing in the ear at night indicates a change of wind

APPETITES

If everything is eaten at the table, it indicates continued clear weather.

ROADS DRYING

When the roads become suddenly dry by wind after heavy rain, expect more within 24 hours.
(C.L. Prince)

ONION SKINS

Onion skins very thin,
Mild Winter coming in;
Onion skins thick and tough,
Coming Winter cold and rough.

COLD FEET

> *Feet tend to go cold before snow*
> (J.W. Jewell)

The feet are the part of the body most sensitive to cold.

OILED FLOORS

Oiled floors become damp before rain.

MATTING SHRINKS

When floor matting shrinks, it is a sign of dry weather; when it expands, expect rain.

STRINGS

Stringed instruments giving forth clear ringing sounds indicate dry weather.

BOILING

When boiling water rapidly evaporates, expect rain.

RUST

If stoves or iron rust during the night, it is a sign of rain.

SOAP

Soap covered with moisture indicates bad weather.

DUST

Dust rising in dry weather signals an approaching change.
Dust whirled around in little eddies by the wind, is a rain sign.

KITES

If kites fly high, fine weather is at hand.

SMOKE DESCENDING

Smoke falling to the ground is a sign of rain within 24 hours.

SPARKS

> *When the sparks stick to the poker, it is a sign of rain.*
> (Spain)

SPRINGS

Springs rise against rain.

CANDLES

When the candle flame spits, flares and snaps, expect rain.

SOOT

If soot falls down the chimney, rain will ensue.

COALS

Coals, burning very bright, foretell wind.
Coals covered with thick white ashes indicate snow in winter and rain in summer.
Coals alternating bright and dim indicate approaching storms.
Burning wood in winter pops more before snow.

FLAMES

If the flames twist and curl, it denotes wind; if paler than usual and murmuring within; it indicates storms approaching.
Fires burn brighter and throw out more heat just before a storm.
Blacksmiths select a stormy day in which to perform work requiring extra heat.
Sunshine is said to put out fire.
A fire hard to kindle indicates bad weather coming.

COFFEE BUBBLES

When bubbles of coffee collect in the centre of the cup, expect fair weather.
When they adhere to the cup, forming a ring, expect rain.
If they separate without assuming any fixed position, expect changeable weather.

THROUGH THE YEAR

JANUARY

FOG

Fog in January makes a wet Spring
Rain in January - full graveyards
The smooth days of January will be paid for in February and March.
A favourable January brings us a good year.
The blackest month in all the year
Is the month of Janiveer.

BRIGHT

In Janiveer if the sun appear,
March and April pay full dear.

MILD

A summerish January, a winterish spring.
If January calends be summerly gay, it will be winterly winter till the calends of May.

WARM

R. Inwards suggests that this means premature growth in vegetation is liable to suffer severe damage from spring frosts.

> *January warm, the Lord have mercy*
> (R. Inwards)

GRAIN

If grain grows in January, there will be a year of great need.

GRASS

If grass grows in Janiveer,
It grows worse for it all year.

FLOWERS

> *January flowers do not fill the granary.*
> (Spain)

BLOSSOMS

> *January blossoms fill no man's cellar.*
> (Portugal)

BIRDS

> *If birds begin to whistle in January, frosts to come.*
> (Rutland)

SPRING

> *A January spring is worth naething.*
> (Scotland)

DRY

Dry January, plenty of wine.

WET

> *A wet January, a wet spring.*
> *A wet January is not so good for corn, but not so bad for cattle.*
> (Spain and Portugal)

January wet, no wine you get.
In January much rain and little snow is bad for mountains, valleys and trees.

THAW

Always expect a thaw in January.

FOG

Fog in January brings a wet spring.

SNOW

> *If there is no snow before January, there will be the more in March and April.*
> *As the day lengthens, so the cold strengthens.*
> *A kindly, good Janiveer freezeth the pot by the fire.*
> (Thomas)

When oak trees bend with snow in January, good crops may be expected.

COLD

A cold January, a feverish February, a dusty March, a weeping April, and a windy May, presage a good year and gay.
(France)

Generals January and February will fight for us.
(Czar Nicholas I)

January, freeze the pot by the fire,
February, fill dyke.
March winds, April showers,
Bring forth May flowers.
March in Janiveer,
Janiveer in March, I fear.

WHOLE YEAR

According to ancient Saxon lore the general trend of the whole year's weather was influenced by the day of the week on which 1st Jan fell, as follows:

	WINTER	*SPRING*	*SUMMER*
MONDAY	Severe/Confused	Good	Windy
TUESDAY	Dreary/Severe	Windy	Rainy
WEDNESDAY	Hard	Bad	Good
THURSDAY	Good	Windy	Good
FRIDAY	Variable	Good	Good
SATURDAY	Snowy	Blowing	Rainy
SUNDAY	Good	Windy	Dry

1ST-3RD:

The first three days of January rule the coming three months.

2ND

As the weather is this day(2nd Jan), so will it be in September.

4TH

> *It will be the same weather for nine weeks as it is on the ninth day after Christmas.*
> (Sweden)

12TH

> *If on the 12th Jan. the sun shine, it foreshows much wind.*
> (Shepherd's Almanack 1676)

14TH - ST HILARYS DAY

> *The coldest day of the year*
> (Yorkshire)

> *January 14th will either be the coldest or wettest day of the year.*
> (Huntingdonshire)

17TH - ST SULPICIUS' DAY

> *Frost on St Sulpicius' Day augers well for the spring*
> (France)

20TH-31ST

The last twelve days of January rule the weather for the whole year.

22ND - ST VINCENT'S DAY

> *If the sun shine brightly on Vincent's Day, We shall have more wine than water.*
> (France)

Remember on St Vincent's Day,
If that the sun his beams display,
Be sure to mark his transient beam,
Which through the casement sheds a gleam;
For 'tis a token bright and clear
Of prosperous weather all the year.

> *If the sun shine on 22nd January, there shall be much wind.*
> (Husbandman's Practice)

> *At St Vincent, all water is as good as seed.*
> (Spain)

> *On St Vincent's Day the sap rises to the branch,*
> *But retires frightened if it finds frost.*
> (France)

If St Vincent has sunshine,
One hopes much rye and wine.

25TH-ST PAUL'S CONVERSION DAY

If St Paul's Day be fine, the year will be the same.
(France)

This festival was called an Egyptian daythere are two unlucky days in each month, so-called Egyptian days, and prognostications of the good or bad course of the year were formed from the state of the weather on these days.
(Du Cange)

If the sun shine on St Paul's Day, it betokens a good year; if rain or snow, indifferent; if misty, it predicts great dearth; if thunder, great winds and death of people that year.
(Shepherds' Almanack 1676)

If Saint Paules be faire and clear
It doth betide a happy year;
But if by chance then it should raine,
It will make deare all kinds of graine.
If the clouds make dark the skie,
The neate and fowles this year shall die;
If blustering winds do blow aloft,
Then wars shall trouble the realm full oft.
(Willsford, Nature's Secrets*)*

Fair on St Paul's Conversion Day is favourable to all fruits. Fair and sunshine. brings fertility to rye and wine.
Paul's Day stormy and windy,
Famine on earth, and much death on people;
Paul's Day beautiful and fair,
Abundance on the earth of corn and meal.
(Isle of Man)

FEBRUARY

FOG

Feb fog means a frost in May

If on Feb. 2, it is bright and clear, the groundhog will stay in his den, indicating that more snow and winter are to come; if it is dark or rainy the winter is over.

If groundhog day is clear, corn and fruits will then be dear.

If it thunders in February, it will frost in April.

TWO-FACED

Double-faced February.

> *Good morrow, Benedict; why, what's the matter,*
> *That you have such a February face,*
> *So full of frost, of storm, of cloudiness?.*
> (Shakespeare, Much Ado About Nothing)

WORST

> *February, the shortest and worst of all the months.*
> (France)

MAD

> *Mad February takes his father into the sunshine and beats him.*
> (Spain)

FINE

There is always one fine week in February.

> *The Welshman had rather see his dam on the bier*
> *Than see a fair Februeer.*
> (Wales)

> *It's better to see a troop of wolves than a fine February.*
> (France)

Isolated fine days in February are known in Surrey as 'weather-breeders', and are considered as certain to be followed by a storm.

BEES

> *If bees get out in February, the next day will be windy and rainy.*
> (Surrey)

> *A February spring is not worth a pin.*
> (Cornwall)

HAY

Warm February, bad hay crop;
Cold February, good hay crop.
All the months of the year
Curse a fair Februeer.

RAIN

> *If in February there be no rain,*
> *'Tis neither good for hay nor grain.*
> (Spain and Portugal)

When it rains in February, it will be temperate all year.
(Spain)

February rain is as good as manure.
(France)

WINDS

Violent north winds in February herald a fertile year.

SNOW

*If February gives much snow,
A fine summer it doth foreshow.*
(France)

END OF MONTH

Whenever the latter part of February and beginning of March are dry, there will be a deficiency of rain up to Midsummer Day.
(C.L. Prince)

When the cat in February lies in the sun, she will creep behind the stove in March. When the north wind does not blow in February, it will surely come in March.

February makes a bridge, and March breaks it
(T. Fuller)

1ST - ST BRIDGET'S DAY, BRIGID, OR BRIDE

As long as the sunbeam comes in on Bridget's feast day, the snow comes before May Day.
(Isle of Man)

2ND - CANDLEMAS

(Purification of Virgin Mary)

On the eve of Candlemas Day
Winter gets stronger or passes away.
(France)

At Candlemas, cold comes to us.
Good weather on this day indicates a long continuance
of winter, and a bad crop; on the contrary, if foul it is a
good omen.
(Isle of Man)

At Candlemas Day
Another winter is on its way.
(France)

If Candlemas Day be fair and clear,
There'll be twa winters in the year.
(Scotland)

If it neither rains nor snows on Candlemas Day
You may straddle your horse and go and buy hay.
(Lincolnshire)

If Candlemas Day be fair and bright,
Winter will have another flight.
But if Candlemas Day bring clouds and rain,
Winter is gone and won't come again..'
On Candlemas day, (also known as Groundhog Day)
the bear, badger or woodchuck comes out to see his
shadow at noon: if he does not see it, he remains out;
but if he does see it, he goes back to his hole for 6

weeks, and cold weather continues for 6 weeks longer.
(United States)

If a storm on 2nd February, spring is near; but if that day be bright and clear, the spring will be late.
If it snows on 2nd February, only so much as may be seen on the back of a black ox, then summer will come soon.
If on 2nd February the goose finds it wet, then the sheep will have grass on 25th March.
When drops hang on the fence on 2nd February, icicles will hang there on 25th March.
When it rains at Candlemas, the cold is over.
(Spain)

If wind's in the east on Candlemas Day,
There it will stick till the 2nd of May.

The earth is said to pass through a swarm of meteors at around this time, as was discovered in the 19th century, bringing unusually cold weather from 5th to 11th February.

6TH - ST DOROTHEA

St Dorothea gives the first snow.

7TH-14TH

Buchan's first cold period.

10TH-28TH

If the eighteen last days of February be Wet, and the first ten of March, you'll see That the spring quarter, and the summer too, Will prove too wet, and danger to ensue.

12TH - ST EULALIE

*If the sun smile on St Eulalie Day,
It is good for apples and cider, they say.*
(France)

12TH TO 14TH

These three days, according to a Highland superstition, are borrowed from January, and it is accounted a good omen if they prove as stormy as possible.

If winter does not pay its debts to December and January it will begin to meet its dues on 12th February.
(France)

Sunshine of St Eulalie" she was called; for that was the sunshine which as the farmers believed, would load their orchards with apples.
(Longfellow, Evangeline)

14TH - ST VALENTINE

To St Valentine, the spring is a neighbour.
(France)

*Winter's back breaks about the middle of February.
The crocus was dedicated to St Valentine, and ought to blossom about this time.*
(Circle of the Seasons)

The third Thursday in February is called the Fair of Auld Deer.

The fair of Auld Deer,
Is the warst day in a' the year.
(Aberdeen)

20TH - 28TH

The nights of this part of February are called in Sweden 'steel nights', on account of their cutting severity.

22ND - ST PETER'S DAY

Spring was at one time considered to begin on St Peter's Day.
If cold at St Peter's Day, it will last longer.
The night of St Peter shows what weather we will have for the next forty days..'

24TH - ST MATHIAS DAY

If it freezes on St Mathias Day, it will freeze for a month together.
St Mathias breaks the ice; if he finds none, he will make it.

28TH - ST ROMANUS

Romanus bright and clear
Indicates a goodly year.

MARCH

When March blows it's horn,
your barn will be filled with hay and corn.

> *March is traditionally a boisterous month throughout the temperate zones of the northern hemisphere. The poles are at their coldest after nearly 6 months of night, and the equator is at its hottest because the sun is overhead.*
> (From R.Inwards)

> *March, many weathers.*
> *March buys winter's cloak and sells it three days afterwards.*
> (France)

In beginning or in end
March its gifts will send.

> *March was so angry with an old woman (according to a saying on the island of Kythnos) for thinking he was a summer month, that he borrowed a day from his brother February, and froze her and her flocks to death.*
> (T. Bent, Greece)

DRY

Dust in March brings dust and foliage.
A dry and cold March never begs its head.
A peck of March dust and a shower in May
Make the corn green and the fields gay.

WET

March dry, good rye;
March wet, good wheat.
(Suffolk)

March never has two days alike.
(France)

SUN

March sun,
Lets snow stand on a stone.
(France)

The March sun wounds. It strikes like a hammer.
(Spain)

WIND

A windy March betokens a bad fish year
March wind wakes the adder and blooms the whin
(Scotland)

March winds and April showers,
Bring forth May flowers.

THUNDER

Thunder in March betokens a fruitful year.
(Germany)

When it thunders in March it brings sorrow.
The morn when first it thunders in March
The eel in the pond gives a leap, they say.
(Browning)

STORMY

March will either come in like a lion and go out like a lamb
Or come in like a lamb and go out like a lion.

VEGETATION

March grows
Never dows (thrives)
  (Yorkshire)

FOGS

Fogs in March,
Frosts in May.
As many fogs in March you see,
So many frosts in May will be.

OTHER MONTHS

As it rains in March, so it rains in June.
As much fog in March, so much rain in summer.
Fog in March, thunder in July.
A wet March makes a sad August.
As much dew in March, so much fog rises in August.
A dusty March, a snowy February, a moist April, and a
dry May preasge a good year.
(France)

1ST - ST DAVID AND ST CHAD

First comes David, then comes Chad,
And then comes Winneral as though he was mad.
(referring to St Winwaloe's Day on the 3rd)

3RD - ST WINWALOE, OR GUENGALOEUS

(Winwaloe was a Breton saint who founded the monastery of Landevenec: died 532AD)

If it does not freeze on the 10th, a fertile year may be expected.

Mists or hoar-frosts on this day betoken a plentiful year, but nor without some diseases.

15TH

> *On March 15th come sun and swallow.*
> (Spain)

17TH - ST PATRICK'S DAY

On St Patrick's Day, the warm side of a stone turns up, and the broad-back goose begins to lay.

19TH - ST JOSEPH'S DAY

Is't on St Joseph's day clear,
So follows a fertile year.

> *When there has been no particular storm about the time of the spring equinox, if a storm arise from the east on or before that day, or if a storm from any point of the compass arise near a week after the equinox, then, in either of these cases, the succeeding summer is*

generally dry, four times in five; but if a storm arise from the south-west or west-south-west on or just before the spring equinox, then the summer following is generally wet, five times in six.
(Dr R Kirwan, Ireland)

21ST - ST. BENOLT

If it rains on the feast of St Benolt it will rain for 40 days after.
(France)

25TH - LADY DAY OR ST MARY'S

Is't on St Mary's bright and clear
Fertile is said to be the year.
The flower cardamine, or lady's-smock, with its milk-white flowers, was dedicated to the Virgin Mary, and appears about Lady Day.

25TH -27TH

High winds on these days, a dry summer to follow.
(Prof. Boerne's Latin MS., 1677-1799)

There are generally some warm days at the end of March or beginning of April, which bring the blackthorn into bloom, and which are followed by a cold period called the blackthorn winter.

28TH-31ST: BORROWED DAYS

March borrowit from April
Three days, and they were ill:
The first was frost, and the second was snaw,

The third was cauld as ever't could blaw.
(Scotland)

The last 3 days of March were called Borrowed Days; for as they are remarked to be unusually stormy, it is feigned that March had borrowed them from April to extend the sphere of his rougher sway.
  (Sir Walter Scott)

The warst blast comes in the borrowing days.

A shepherd promised March a lamb if he would temper the winds to suit his flocks; but after gaining his point, the shepherd refused to pay over the lamb. In revenge March borrowed three days from April, in which fiercer winds than ever blew and punished the deceiver.
(Spain and a similar legend in Scotland and N England, as follows.

March said to Averill
I see three hoggs on yonder hill
An' if ye'll lend me dayis three
I'll find a way to gar them dee.
The first o' them was snaw an' sleet;
The third o' them was sic' a freeze,
It froze the birds' nebs to the trees.
When the three days were past and gane,
The silly hoggs cam' hirplin hame.

APRIL

EASTER

Rain on Easter Sunday, it will rain the next 7 Sundays.

> *April snow breeds grass*
> *Till April's dead,*
> *Change not a thread.*

> *April showers bring May flowers*

> *A dry April*
> *Not the farmer's will.*
> *April wet*
> *Is what he would get.*

> *Whatever March does not want, April brings along.*

> *April and May are the keys of the year.*
> (Spain)

RAIN

> *In April each drop counts for a thousand.*
> (Spain)

> *April has 30 days: if it rained on 31 no harm would be done*
> (France)

April showers bring summer flowers.
An April flood carries away the frog and his brood.

THUNDER

Thunderstorm in April is the end of hoar-frost.

> *When April blows his horn*
> *it's good for hay and corn.*
> (Isle of Man)

CHANGEABLE

Changeable as an April day,

> *The uncertain glory of an April day.*
> (Shakespeare)

April weather
Rain and sunshine, both together.

SNOW

Snow in March devours: snow in April is manure.

> *April snow stays no longer than water on a trout's back.*
> (Wales)

April snow breeds grass.

WIND

A windy April is death to little pigs.

FOGS

> *Fogs in April foretell a wheat-crop failure next year.*
> (Alabama)

1ST - APRIL FOOL'S DAY

If it thunders on April Fool's Day
It brings good crops of corn and hay.

1ST-3RD

If the first three days of April be foggy,
There will be a flood in June.
(Huntingdon)

If the first three days of April be foggy
Rain in June will make the lanes boggy.

5TH - ST VINCENT OF SPAIN

If St Vincent's Day is fair, there will be more water than wine.
(France)

6TH - LATTER LADY DAY

On Lady Day the latter
The cold comes on the water..'
(T. Fuller)

11TH - 14TH

Formerly known as 'Buchan's second cold period.'

23RD - ST GEORGE

If it rains on St. George's Day he eats all the cherries.
(France)

25TH - ST MARK

> *Rain on St. Marks Day augurs ill for fruit.*
> (France)

As long before St Marks Day as the frogs are heard croaking, so long will they keep quiet afterwards.

MAY

A cold May gives full barns and empty churchyards.
The merry month of May.

> *Welcome be thou, faire freshhe May.*
> (Chaucer)

WARM

> *Heat in May gives strength to the whole year.*
> (France)

A hot May makes a fat churchyard.

COLD

> *A cold May is kindly; and fills the barn finely*
> (Scotland, England)

> *In the middle of May comes the tail of winter.*
> (France)

> *A cold May gives full barns and empty churchyards.*
> (Wales)

RAIN

To be hoped for, like rain in May.
Rain in the beginning of May is said to injure the wine.

> *A wet May makes a big load of hay.*
> (West Shropshire)

THUNDER

The more thunder in May, the less in August and September.

> *Maids are May when they are maids; but the sky changes when they are wives.*
> (Shakespeare, As You Like It)

SNOW

A snow storm in May is worth a wagon-load of hay.

AND OTHER MONTHS

> *A cold May and a hot June send bread and wine.*
> (France)

> *A leaking May and a warm June bring on the harvest very soon.*
> (Scotland)

> *Wet May means a dry July.*
> (Germany)

> *If May be cold and wet, September will be warm and dry, and vice versa.*
> (C.L. Prince)

A first of May hoar-frost
Promises a good harvest.

The later the blackthorn in bloom after 1st May, the better the rye and harvest.

8TH

> *If on the 8th of May it rain,*
> *It foretells a wet harvest, men slain.*
> (T. Fuller)

9TH - 14TH

Buchan's third cold period.

11TH - ST MAMMERTUS

12TH - ST PANCRAS

13TH - ST SERVATIUS

These three days are known as the festivals of the 'Ice Saints' or 'Ice Men'

> *St Mammertus, St Pancras, and St Servatius do not pass without frost.*
> (France)

ST SERVATIUS DAY

Who shears his sheep before St Servatius Day loves more his wool than his sheep.
About this day it is unusually cold, blamed, in the 19th century by Prof Erman of Berlin on a swarm of meteors through which earth passes.

17TH - 19TH

The three days in which St Dunstan was said to have bartered his soul with the devil, causing frosts.
He is alleged to have set up business as a brewer and to have

struck a deal with the devil to cause frosts to destroy the rival cider crop. It was agreed, so the story goes, that the arch-enemy should keep his part of the bargain in perpetuity, ending on St Dunstan's Day, 19th May. In the apple-growing districts of north Devon the same legend is told of one Franklin, but the dates there are 19th - 21st May, which are known as 'St Franklin's days.'

17TH - 23RD:

> *If storms from the east or south-east, between 17th and 23rd May, this indicates a wet summer.*
> (Prof. Boerne's Latin MS 1677-1799)

19TH - ST DUNSTAN'S DAY

> *Easterly winds on 19th - 21st May indicate a dry summer.*
> (Prof. Boerne's Latin MS 1677-1799)

25TH - ST URBAN'S DAY

26TH - ST PHILIPS' DAY

At one time in the Middle Ages, St Urban's Day was regarded as the first day of summer.

> *When it rains on St Philip's Day, the poor will not need help from the rich.*
> (France, ref. St Philip Neri of Florence, 1515-95)

JUNE

If June be sunny, harvest comes early.

In the hay season, when there is no dew, it indicates rain.

> *It is a good June that brings some rain and some dry weather*
> (Wales)

WINDS

When the wind goes to the west early in June, expect wet weather till the end of August.

If north wind blows in June, good rye harvest.

CALM

Calm weather in June
Sets corn in tune
June damp and warm
Does the farmer no harm
A dripping June
Sets all things in tune.

RAIN

A cold and wet June spoils the rest of the year.

> *June rain brings ruin to the mill.*
> (France)

HARVEST

In Scotland an early harvest is expected when the bramble blossoms early in June.

AND OTHER MONTHS

When it is hottest in June, it will be coldest in the corresponding days of the next February.

A wet June makes a dry September.
(Cornwall)

8TH - ST MEDARD

If on the 8th of June it rain,
It foretells a wet harvest, men sain.

If it rains on the 8th of June
It will rain after, for 40 days;
The same is said of the 19th June
That day given to St Protase.

11TH - ST BARNABAS DAY

Rain on St Barnabas Day is good for grapes.
On St Barnabas Day, the sun has come to stay.
(Spain)

15TH - ST VITUS'S DAY

If St Vitus's Day be rainy weather
It will rain for 30 days together.
Oh! St Vitus, do not rain, so that we may not want barley.

20TH - MIDSUMMER EVE

If it rains on Midsummer Eve, the filberts will be spoiled.

21ST

If Midsummer Day be never so little rainy, the hazel and walnut will be scarce; corn smitten in many places; but apples, pears, and plums will not be hurt.
(Shepherd's Kalendar)

24TH - ST JOHN'S DAY

Before St John's Day we pray for rain; after that we get it anyhow.
Rain on St John's day and we may expect a wet harvest.
Rain on St John's day, damage to nuts.

27TH

If it rains on 27th June, it will rain seven weeks.

29TH - 4TH JULY

Buchan's fourth cold period.

JULY

Corn knee high by the fourth of July,
you'll have a good supply

If ant hills are high in July,
Winter will be snowy

When the sun enters Leo, the greatest heat will then arise.

> *Ne'er trust a July sky*
> (Shetland)

THUNDER

Much thunder in July injures wheat and barley.

CALM

July, God send thee calm and fayre,
That happy harvest we may see,
With quyet tyme and healthsome ayre,
and man to God may thankful bee.

No tempest, good July
Lest the corn look ruely.

RAIN

A shower of rain in July, when the corn begins to fill,
Is worth a plough of oxen, and all belongs theretill.

AND OTHER MONTHS

As July, so the next January.

Whatever July and August do not boil, September cannot fry.

When the months of July, August and September are unusually hot, January will be the coldest month.

1ST

If the 1st of July it be rainy weather,
It will rain more or less for four weeks together.

2ND

> *If it rains on 2nd July, the Visitation Day of St Mary, it will rain for twenty days.*
> (Denmark)

3RD - 11TH DOG-DAYS

> *As the Dog-days commence, so they end.*
> *If it rains on first Dog-day, it will rain for forty days after.*
> *The period of greatest summer heat, lasting around 3rd July - 11th August, was called by the ancient Romans caniculares dies, because they wrongly supposed that Sirius, the Dog Star and the brightest star in the sky, which then rose and set approximately with the sun at that season, reinforced the power of the solar rays and so caused the wesather to be at its warmest. We now know that all the stars together don not send even one ten-millionth part as much heat as it gets from the sun.*
> (from R Inwards)

Dog-days bright and clear
Indicate a happy year;

But when accompanied by rain,
For better times our hopes are vain.

4TH - ST MARTIN BULLION'S DAY

If Bullion's Day be fine, there will be a good harvest.
(Scotland)

The cult of the festival of St Martin was brought to Scotland by the Normans, as St Martin le Boillant, to distinguish it from Martinmas, St Martin of the Winter (11th November). The fourth of July was set as the date of the ordination and translation of the saint.

Bullion's Day, gif ye bring rain
For forty days it will remain.
Bullion's Day, gif ye be fair,
For forty days 'twill rain nae mair.
(Northern Scotland)

If the deer rise and lie down on Bullion's Day, there will be a good go-harvest.
(Scotland)

5TH

The first Friday in July is always wet..
(C.W. Empson, Folklore Journal)

10TH

If it rains on 10th July, it will rain for seven weeks.

12TH - 15TH

Buchan's first warm period.

15TH - ST SWITHIN'S DAY

> *St Swithin's Day, if ye do rain,*
> *For forty days it will remain;*
> *St Swithin's day, an ye be fair,*
> *For forty days 'twill rain nae mair.*
> (Scotland)

The legend goes that St Swithin, Bishop of Winchester and a builder (died 862) was buried at his own request outside the church "in a vile and unworthy place" under the drip of the eaves so the sweet rain of heaven might fall upon his grave. A century later it was decided, on 15th July, to move his remains to the interior of the church. By way of protest the saint arranged for a forty-day deluge, causing the monks to abandon the project.

If it rains on 15th July, the saying goes that 'St Swithin is christening the apples.

It is said in Tuscany that the weather on St Gallo's Day (15th July) will prevail for forty days; and at Rome the period is extended to any day within the octave of St Bartholomew (24th August).

All the tears that St Swithin can cry
St. Bartlemy's dusty mantle wipes dry.

19TH - ST VINCENT'S DAY

20TH - ST MARGARET'S DAY

At St Vincent the rain ceases and the wind comes.
(France)

Rain on St Margaret's day will destroy all kinds of nuts.
(Germany)

22ND - ST MARY MAGDALENE

Referring to the wet weather prevalent about mid-July, the saying is 'St Mary Magdalene is washing her handkerchief to go to her cousin St James's fair.'
(Folklore Journal)

26TH - ST ANNE'S DAY

If it rains on this day it will rain for one month and one week.
(France)

27TH - ST GODELIEVE

If it rains on this day it will rain for forty days after
(Belgium)

THE SUNNIEST PLACES IN THE UK*	
St Helier (Jersey)	St Peter Port (Guernsey)
Shanklin (IOW)	Sandown (IOW)
Ventnor (IOW)	Worthing (Sussex)
Eastbourne (Sussex)	Hastings (Sussex)
Littlehampton (Sussex)	Hayling Island (Hants)
Weymouth (Dorset)	Ryde (IOW)
Folkestone (Kent)	

* Courtesy of the British Weather Centre

AUGUST

If the first week in August is unusually warm,
the coming Winter will be snowy and long.
For every fog in August,
There will be a snowfall in Winter.
If a cold August follows a hot July,
It foretells a Winter hard and dry.
Dry August and warm, doth harvest no harm

THUNDER

> *August thunder promises fat grapes and fine vintages.*
> (France)

Thunderstorms in the beginning of August will generally be followed by others all the month.

SUN

> *Red sun in August, rain everywhere.*
> (France)

RAIN

> *August rain gives honey, wine and saffron.*
> (Portugal)

> *When it rains in August, it rains honey and wine.*
> (France and Spain)

> *A wet August never brings dearth.*
> (Italy)

FOG

A fog in August indicates a severe winter and plenty of snow.
As many August fogs; so many winter mists.

> *Observe on what day in August the first heavy fog occurs, and expect a hard frost on the same day in October.*
> (United States)

DEW

When the dew is heavy in August, the weather generally remains fair.

AND OTHER MONTHS

As August, so the next February.

> *August ripens; September gathers in;*
> *August bears the burden; September the fruit..*
> (Portugal)

None in August should over the land,
In December none over the sea.

1ST - LAMMAS DAY

After Lammas, corn ripens as much by night as by day.
Lammas was Hlafmas the loaf mass, bread or corn mass. Lammas-floods are traditional in Scotland, and indeed August is normally the wettest month of the twelve over much of that country.
If the first week of August is unusually warm, the winter will be white and long..'

6TH - 11TH

Buchan's fifth cold period

9TH - ST LAWRENCE'S DAY

> *If on St Lawrence's Day the weather be fine, fair autumn and good wine may be hoped for.*
> (Germany)

The 10th August is another suggested cold period due to the earth supposedly passing through a meteor shower.

12TH - 15TH

Buchan's second warm period

23RD - ST BARTHOLOMEW'S DAY

> *At Bartholomew,*
> *There comes a cold dew.*
> (Huntingdon)

At one time during the Middle Ages St. Bartholomew's Day was regarded as inaugurating autumn.

At St Bartholomew's Day, so the whole autumn.
If Bartlemy's Day be fair and clear,
They hope for a prosperous autumn that year.

> *If the 24th be misty, the morning beginning with a hoarfrost, the cold weather will soon come, and a hard winter.*
> (Shepherd's Kalendar)

If it rains this day, it will rain forty days after.
(Rome)

Thunderstorms after Bartholomew's Day are more violent.

SEPTEMBER

September dries up ditches or breaks down bridges.
(Portugal)

THUNDER

Thunder in September indicates a good crop of grain and fruit for next year.

If September storms clear off warm, all the following winter's storms will be warm.

SUN

Tis September's sun which causes the black list upon the antelope's back.
(Bombay)

RAIN

A wet September, drought for next summer, famine, and no crops.
(California)

Heavy September rains bring drought.
(United States)

Rain in September is good for the farmer, but poison to the vine-growers.
(Germany)

September rain is much liked by the farmer.

COLD

When a cold spell occurs in September and passes without a frost, a frost will not occur until the same time in October.

AND OTHER MONTHS

As September, so the next March.
September is autumn's May.
(France)

When September has been rainy, the following May is generally dry; and when May is dry, the following September is apt to be wet.
(Prof. Boerne's Latin MS., 1677-1799)

September blow soft till the fruit's in the loft.
November take flail, let ships no more sail.

1ST

Fair on 1st September; fair for the month.

8TH

As on the 8th September; so for the next 4 weeks.

13TH

When 13th of September falls on a Friday, the autumn will be dry and sunny.
(France)

14TH – HOLYROOD, OR ROOD DAY

The passion flower blooms around this time. The flower is said to resemble the cross or rood, the nails, and the crown of thorns, used at the Crucifixion.
(from Circle of The Seasons)

If dry be the buck's horn
on Holyrood morn
'Tis worth a kist of gold
But if wet it be seen
Ere Holyrood e'en
Bad harvest is foretold.
(Yorkshire)

If the hart and hind meet dry and part dry on Rood day fair,
For sax weeks, of rain there'll be nae mair.
(Scotland)

Wild with the wind of September
Wrestled the trees of the forest.
(Longfellow)

There are generally three consecutive windy days around mid-September which have been called by Midland farmers 'the windy days of barley harvest.

This day is said to be fine in six years out of seven.
(T Forster, Perennial Calendar, 1824)

19TH

If on the 19th September there is a storm from the south, a mild winter can be expected.
(Derby)

20th, 21st and 22nd of September, these three days, rule the weather for October, November and December.

21ST - ST. MATHEW'S

On St Mathew's day, rain fattens pigs and goats.
(Spain)

Mathew's Day bright and clear
Brings good wine in next year.
South wind on 21st September indicates that the rest of the autumn will be warm.
St Mathews
Brings on the cold dew.

22ND - AUTUMN EQUINOX

A quiet week before the autumn equinox and after, the temperature will continue higher than usual into the winter.

29TH - ST MICHAELMAS'S DAY

As many days old the Moon is on Michaelmas day, so many floods after.
(Howell)

If Michaelmas day be fair, the sun will shine much in the winter, though the wind at north-east will frequently reign long and be very sharp and nipping.

On Michaelmas day, the devil puts his foot on the blackberries.
(North of Ireland)

If St Michael brings many acorns, Christmas will cover the fields with snow.
St Michael's rain does not stay long in the sky.
Michaelmas rain without a storm foretells a mild winter.
(France)

At Michaelmas the heat goes into the sky.
(France)

If it does not rain on St Michaels's and Gallus, a dry spring is indicated for the next year.

OCTOBER

When leaves fall early,
Fall and Winter will be mild;
When leaves fall late,
Winter will be severe.

Much rain in October,
Much wind in December.

A warm October,
A cold February.

Full Moon in October without frost,
No frost 'till November's Full Moon.

This, our golden month,
October.
(Young)

October's gold is dim
The forests rot.
(Gray)

THUNDER

Thunder in October brings good vintages.
(France)

WIND

A good October and a good blast,
To blow the hog acorn and mast.

LEAVES

If in the fall of the leaves in October many of them wither on the boughs and hangre there, it betokens a frosty winter and much snow.

FINE

> *There are always nineteen (some say twenty-one) fine days in October.*
> (Kent)

FOG

For every fog in October, a snow in winter, heavy or light according as how the fog is heavy or light.

> *October fogs and November rains bring heaven's blessings.*
> (France)

FROSTS

If October bring heavy frosts and winds, then will January and February be mild.

RAIN

Much rain in October, much wind in December.

COLD

When it freezes and snows in October, January will bring mild weather; but if it is thundering and heat-lightning, the weather will resemble April in temper.

October and November cold indicate that the following January and February will be mild and dry.
(C.L Prince)

BIRDS AND BADGERS

When the birds and badgers are fat in October, expect a cold winter.
(United States)

SNOW

If the first snow falls on moist soft earth, it indicates a small harvest; but if upon hard, frozen soil, a good harvest.

FULL MOON

Full Moon in October without frost, no frost till Full Moon in November.

AND OTHER MONTHS

Warm October, cold February.

As October, so the following March.

2ND

Full Moon in October without frost, no frost 'til Full Moon in November.

16TH - GALLUS

Dry on Gallus means a dry spring the next year.

18TH - ST LUKE'S DAY

This day is 'St Luke's little summer', so-called as there is often about this time a spell of dry, fine weather.

28TH - ST JUDE'S DAY

> *On St Jude's day*
> *The oxen may play.*
> *November take flail,*
> *Let ships no more sail.*
> (Tusser)

> *St Jude's Day was anciently accounted as certain to be rainy. The saying is not literally true, but it expresses recognition of a fact brought to light by modern statistics. By official averages, October's last week is the wettest of the year in Southern England. The chances of a completely dry day are at a minimum about 28th October*
> (from R. Inwards).

NOVEMBER

Ice in November to bear a duck,
The rest of the winter'll be slush and muck

If the November goose bone be thick, so will the winter weather be; If the non-goose bone be thin, so will the winter weather be.

Flowers bloomin' in late Autumn,
A sure sign of a bad Winter comin'.

A warm November is the sign of a bad Winter

No warmth, no cheerfulness, no healthful ease,
No comfortable feel in any member,
No shade, no shine, no butterflies, no bees,
No fruits, no flowers, no leaves, no birds - no-vember.
(T.Hood)

November's sky is shill and drear.
(Scott)

Thunder in November, a fertile year to come.
Thunder in November on the Northern Lakes is taken as a sign that the lakes will remain open till at least the middle of December.
(United States)

When in November the water rises, it will show itself the whole winter.
A heavy November snow will last till April.
(New England)

As November, so the following March.

1ST NOV - 'ALL SAINTS' DAY', OR 'HALLOWMAS'

If this day be fair, the next winter will bring but little rain and snow along with it; but if this day be clear and the other cloudy, the beginning of winter will accordingly be fair, but its end and spring will turn out rigorous and disagreeable.
(Kalm)

There is often about this time some warm weather, called The All Saints' Rest.
(Sweden)

Farewell, thou latter spring; farewell, thou All Hallow'n summer.
(Shakespeare. Henry 1v)

These refer to the short period of unseasonable warmth that often comes to Western and Northern Europe. In England the tradition of such a warm spell appears to have died out in Shakespeare's time, but remains current in Scandinavia.

If ducks do slide at Hallontide,
At Christmas they will swim;
If ducks do swim at Hallontide,
At Christmas they will slide.
(Hallontide = Hallowen-tide.)
From All Saints' Day to the end of Advent there can never be too much rain or wind.
(France)

If on All Saints Day the beech nut be found dry, we shall have a hard winter, but if the nut be wet and not light, we may expect a wet winter.

If All Saints' Day will bring out the winter, St Martin's Day (the 11th of November) will bring out Indian summer.
(United States)

6TH - 13TH

Buchan's sixth cold period.

11TH - ST MARTIN OR MARTINMAS

If it is at Martinmas, fair, dry and cold; the cold in winter will not last long.
If the geese at Martin's Day stand on ice, they will walk in mud at Christmas.
If the leaves of the trees and grapevines do not fall before St Martin's Day, a cold winter may be expected.
Wind north-west at Martinmas; severe winter to come.
(Huntingdonshire)

If the wind is in the south-west at Martinmas, it keeps there till after Candlemas (Feb. 2nd), with a mild winter up to then and no snow to speak of.
(Midland Counties)

At St Martin's Day, winter is on his way
(France)

Expect St Martin's summer, halcyon days (i.e. fine weather at Martinmas)
(Shakespeare Henry VI)

St Martin's summer lasts for 3 days and a bit.
(France)

THE LEGEND OF ST MARTIN

One bleak early November morning St Martin, Bishop of Tours, gave half his cloak to a poor man shivering from the cold. Seeing this, the Good Lord set the sun shining warmly until the saint could get himself another garment. Thus was ordained a spell of fair and mild weather to evermore occur in early November.

> *Where the wind is on Martinmas Eve, there it will be for the coming winter.*
> (Old saying in Atherstone)

The weather on Martinmas Eve was anxiously watched by Midland County farmers, as it was supposed to be an index to the barometer for some two or three months for war

21ST

As November 21st, so is the winter.

23RD NOV - ST CLEMENT'S DAY

At one time during the Middle Ages, St Clement's Day was regarded as inaugurating winter.

25TH - ST. CATHERINE

As at Catherine foul or fair, so will be the next February.

26TH - ST VINCENT'S DAY

On St Vincent's day, winter waxes or wanes.
(France)

DECEMBER

December's frost and January's flood,
Never boded the husbandman's good.

Thunder in December,
Presages fine weather.

December cold with snow,
good for rye.

Squirrels gathering nuts in a flurry,
Will cause snow to gather in a hurry.

As high as the weeds grow,
So will the bank of snow.

A green Christmas;
A white Easter.

If there's thunder during Christmas week,
The Winter will be anything but meek.

A tough Winter is ahead if:
- corn husks are thick and tight.
- apple skins are tough.
- birds migrate early.
- squirrels tails are very bushy.
- berries and nuts are plentiful.
- bees build their nests high in the trees.

If the breast bone of the Thanksgiving goose is red or has many spots, expect a cold and stormy Winter; but if only a few spots are visible, expect a mild Winter.

The severity of Winter is determined by how far down the feathers have grown on a partridge's leg.

The wider the brown (middle) band on a woolly bear caterpillar, the milder the Winter.

The nearer the New Moon to Christmas Day, the harder the Winter.

If the first snowfall lands on unfrozen ground, the Winter will be mild.

On the first Sunday of December, if it rains before Mass, it will rain for a week.

7TH - ST AMBROSE

> *At the feast of St Ambrose, cold weather comes for 8 days.*
> (France)

11TH

> *The fourteen **halcyon days** then began - days in which in the Mediterranean calm weather was expected, so that the halcyon, or kingfisher, could (it was supposed) make its nest among rocks close by the brink of the sea.*
> (Virgil-Georgics Bk1, line 393)

The halcyon was a fabled bird identified with the kingfisher, that was supposed to have had the magical power to calm the wind and the waves during the winter solstice while it rested on the sea. Nowadays it refers to any days of fine weather occurring near the winter solstice, but originally it was held specifically to be seven days before and seven days after.

13TH

The last of the unusually cold days said to be the result of earth passing through a meteor shower.

21ST - ST THOMAS'S DAY

We were told to look at the weathercock on St Thomas's Day at twelve o'clock and see which way the wind was, for there it was said it would stick for the next (lunar) quarter..

22ND - WINTER SOLSTICE

Frost on the shortest day is said to indicate a severe winter.
(Lancashire)

25TH

If windy on Christmas Day, trees will bring much fruit.
The twelve days from 25th Dec.-5th January were said to be the keys of the weather for the whole year.

26TH - ST STEPHEN'S DAY

St Stephen's Day windy, bad for next year's grapes.

28TH - INNOCENTS' DAY OR CHILDERMAS

If it be lowering and wet on Childermas Day there will be scarcity; whereas if the day be fair it promises plenty.
(The Shepherd's Kalendar)

31ST

If New Year's Eve night wind blow south,
 It betokeneth warmth and growth;
 If west, much milk, and fish in the sea;
 If north, much cold and storms there will be;
 If east, the trees will bear much fruit;
 If north-east, flee it man and brute.

APPENDIX

THE STORY OF THE SEASONS OF ARNHEM LAND

Northern Territories, Australia

The table portrays the wisdom of the Milingimbi, people truly in touch with their land, in that the dynamics of the weather, the cycle of life on the earth and the view of the heavens are as one with the changing of seasons.

Most grasses are seeding in Midawarr, the season of fruiting plants. Dhimurru, the east wind signals the beginning of the time of abundant food. Midawarr is the season that everyone looks forward to. There is an abundance of food in Midawarr and the daily storms and strong winds are nearly over.

Burra, the northwest wind gives way to Lungurrma, the

northeast wind early in Midawarr, bringing rough seas and heavy waves which crash onto the shore. Early in the season the storms still bring heavy rain daily, often with thunder and lightning. Insects are noticeably absent. The deep sea is heavy and rolls with big waves. By the middle of Midawarr, the wind has changed to Dhimurru, the east wind and the heavy storms are less frequent. Light easterly winds blow throughout most of the day, bringing cooler weather, which is welcomed after the humid weather of the early wet season. With the break in the rain, insects quickly set about their work. Ants busily rebuild nests in the soft soil, while wasps collect soft mud for their nests.

When the mango trees shoot new leaves which are red, the first southeast wind blows. This wind is called Bulunu. In Midawarr it gently blows early in the morning, before sunrise. Then, shortly after sunrise, Dhimurru, the east wind blows and continues for the rest of the day. The seas are very flat at this time and it is often hard to see where the sea ends and the sky starts, because the horizon is lost in the reflection of the sky shown on the sea. This is the time for turtle hunting.

The clouds are still large and vertical and growing higher during the day, just like the storm clouds of early Midawarr. In the evening, clouds of middle and late Midawarr are yellow and red and glow after sunset while the stars begin to shine in clear air. Midawarr is the season of fruiting plants. In Burramirri, the early part of the wet season the bush was thick with plant growth. Then the green growth was sprinkled with colourful flowers in Mayaltha, the season of flowering plants. Now, these same plants are fruiting. During Midawarr, the fruit grows until finally, a few weeks before the end of Midawarr, most fruits are ripe. This is a special time called Nathanamukulinamirri, which simply means 'harvest time'.

The Milingimbi Literature Production Centre,
Northern Territory, Australia

FULL MOON NAMES AND THEIR MEANINGS

(courtesy; The Farmers Almanac)

Native American tribes kept track of the seasons by giving names to each full Moon. In general the same names used throughout tribes from New England to Lake Superior. Full Moon dates shift from year to year and there are 13, as each lunation is approximately 29.5 days long.

JANUARY; FULL WOLF MOON

Also Old Moon, Moon After Yule and sometimes Full Snow Moon. Amid the cold and deep snows of midwinter, the wolf packs howled hungrily outside Indian villages.

FEBRUARY; FULL SNOW MOON

Also Hunger Moon, Wolf Moon and Snow Moon. Named because the heaviest snow usually falls during this month, harsh weather conditions made hunting very difficult.

MARCH; FULL WORM MOON

Also Sap, Full Sap, Crow, Full Crow, and Lenten Moon. Considered to be the last full Moon of winter. As the temperature begins to warm and the ground begins to thaw, earthworm casts appear, heralding the return of the robins. 'Full Crow' Moon, refers to the cawing of crows that signalled the end of winter; 'Full Crust', because the snow cover becomes crusted from thawing by day and freezing at night, and 'Full Sap', marks the time of tapping maple trees.

APRIL; FULL PINK MOON

Also Full Sprouting Grass Moon, the Egg Moon, and among

coastal tribes the Full Fish Moon, because this was the time that the shad swam upstream to spawn. This name came from the herb moss pink, or wild ground phlox, which is one of the earliest widespread flowers of the spring.

MAY; FULL FLOWER MOON

Also Full Corn Planting Moon, or the Milk Moon. In most areas, flowers are abundant everywhere during this time.

JUNE; FULL STRAWBERRY MOON

Also Flower and Strawberry Moon. This name was universal to every Algonquin tribe. However, in Europe they called it the Rose Moon.

JULY; THE FULL BUCK MOON

July is normally the month when the new antlers of buck deer push out of their foreheads in coatings of velvety fur. It was also often called the Full Thunder Moon, for the reason that thunderstorms are most frequent during this time. Another name was the Full Hay Moon.

AUGUST; FULL STURGEON MOON

The fishing tribes are given credit for the naming of this Moon, since sturgeon, a large fish of the Great Lakes and other major bodies of water, were most readily caught during this month. A few tribes knew it as the Full Red Moon because, as the Moon rises, it appears reddish through any sultry haze. It was also called the Green Corn Moon or Grain Moon.

SEPTEMBER; FULL HARVEST MOON

This is the full Moon that occurs closest to the autumn equinox. In two years out of three, the Harvest Moon comes in September, but in some years it occurs in October. The names Fruit and Barley were reserved only for those years when the Harvest Moon is very late in September. At the peak of harvest, farmers can work late into the night by the light of this Moon. Usually the full Moon rises an average of 50 minutes later each night, but for the few nights around the Harvest Moon, the Moon seems to rise at nearly the same time each night: just 25 to 30 minutes later across the U.S., and only 10 to 20 minutes later for much of Canada and Europe. Corn, pumpkins, squash, beans, and wild rice the chief Indian staples are now ready for gathering.

OCTOBER; FULL HUNTER'S MOON

With the leaves falling and the deer fattened, it is time to hunt. Since the fields have been reaped, hunters can easily see fox and the animals which have come out to glean.

NOVEMBER; FULL BEAVER MOON

This was the time to set beaver traps before the swamps froze, to ensure a supply of warm winter furs. Another interpretation suggests that the name Full Beaver Moon comes from the fact that the beavers are now actively preparing for winter. It is sometimes also referred to as the Frosty Moon.

DECEMBER: THE FULL COLD MOON; OR THE FULL LONG NIGHTS MOON

During this month the winter cold fastens its grip, and nights are at their longest and darkest. It is also sometimes called the

Moon before Yule. The term Long Night Moon is a doubly appropriate name because the midwinter night is indeed long, and because the Moon is above the horizon for a long time. The midwinter full Moon has a high trajectory across the sky because it is opposite a low Sun. Also called Moon Before Yule.

BIBLIOGRAPHY

Abercromby, R., and W. Marriot, *Popular Weather Prognostics,*(Paper in *Journal of Royal Meteorological Society,* Vol ix, No.49
A Descant Upon Weather Wisdom. Anon. London 1790
Alcock, H., *The Lunar Effect,* Moana, 1989
Allan, W., *Weather Wisdom from January to December,* London
Animal Weatherlore in America, article in *Knowledge,* April 1886
Atkinson, B., The Werather Business, Aldus, 1968
Bardens, D., Psychic Animals, Capall Bann, 1987
Bassett, F., *Legends and Superstitions of the Sea and Sailors,* London 1885
BBC Weather centre
Bohn, H.G., *Handbook of Proverbs,* London 1855
Brooks, C.F., *Why The Weather?* London 1935
Burke, V.R., *Sancho Panza's Proverbs,* 1872
Canu, F., *Manuel de Meteorological Agricole,* Paris 1884
Chambers, G.F., *The Story of The Weather,* London 1897
Chambers, G.F., *Weather Facts and Predictions,* London 1877
Chambers, R., *Book of Days,* London 1897
Chambers, R., *Popular Rhymes of Scotland,* London 1847
Claridge, J, *Rules To Judge The Changes in Weather,* London 1764
Clouston, Rev. C., *An Explanation of the Popular Weather Prognostics of Scotland,* Edinburgh 1867
Collins, J., *Dictionary of Spanish Proverbs,* 1823
Criswick, H.T.C., *The Agriculturists Weather Guide,* London 1863
Denham, M.A., *Proverbs and Popular Sayings, Relating To Seasons.1846*
Dickson, H.N., *Weather Folklore of Scottish Fishermen,* (Journal of Scottish Meteorological Society, No.6, 1888

Drome, M., *Prediction du Temps,* Paris 1862

Dudgeon,P., *List of Proverbs,* (Folklore Record) Vol. iv, p.127

Dunwoody, H., *Weather Proverbs,* US. War Dept., Washington 1883

Dyer, T.F., *English Folklore,* London 1884

Empson, C., *List of Weather Proverbs,* Folklore Record, Vol.iv.p127

Fisheries Museum of the Atlantic

Folley, T., The Book Of The Moon, Courage 1997

Forster, T., *Pocket Encyclopaedia of Natural Phenomena,* London

Forster, T., *Researches about Atmospheric Phenomena,* London 1823

Forster, T., *The Perennial Calendar,* London 1824

Fryer, J., *Weatherwise,* Bristol 1846

Geocities, Yahoo.com

Gerard, J., *The Herbal or General History of Plants,* London, 1597

Giles, B., The Story of Weather, *UK Weather Centre* Gomis, D., *Folklore Catala,* Barcelona 1888

Griffiths, R., *Welsh Weather Proverbs,* Paper to Welsh Naturalists Society, March, 1894

Gutch, J., *Quarterly Journal of Meteorology,* London 1843

Hardy, Wright and co., The Weather Book, Michael Joseph, 1982

Hawke, B., *Buchan's Days,* London, 1937

Hawke, E., *Weather Lore: as compiled by Richard Inwards,* London, 1950

Heap, G., *The Weather and Climatic Changes,* London, 1879

Heath, R., A Key To Stonehenge, Bluestone Press, 1993

Henderson, J., *Meteorography,* 1841

Holford, I., *Guiness Book of Weather facts and Feats,* Guiness Superlatives, 1977

Hone's Works, *Every-day Book, Table Book, and Year Book,* London, 1839

Humphreys, W., *Rain Making and Other Weather Vagaries,* Baltimore 1926

Humphreys, W., *Weather Proverbs and Paradoxes,* Baltimore 1934

Husbandman's Practice, London, 1663

Inwards, R., Weather Lore, Rider and Co, 1893

Jackson, Gainor, Settlement By Sail, GP Pub., 1991

Jackson, Georgina, *Shropshire Folklore,* London, 1883

Jenyns, Rev. L., *Observations in Meteorology,* London, 1848

Jenyns, Rev. L., *St Swithin and other Weather Saints,* Bath, 1871

Kerner von Marilaun, *Natural History of Plants,* 1895

Knox-Johnston, R., Beyond Jules Verne

Lamb, J., *Aratus: The Phenomena and Diosemeia,* London 1848

Lowe, E., *A Treatise on Atmospheric Phenomena,* London, 1846

Lowe, E., *Prognostications of the Weather,* London, 1849

Mann, R.,*The Weather,* London, 1827

Maudsley, A., *Nature's Weather Warnings,* London, 1891

Meagre, L., *The New Art of Gardening,* 1697

Merle, Rev, W.,*The Earliest Known Journal of the Weather 1337-1344,* London, 1891

Mills, J.,*An Essay on the Weather,* London, 1773

Murphy, P., *Meteorology,* London, 1836

National Geographic

Northall, G., *English Folk-Rhymes,* London, 1892

Northern Florida Amateur Radio Service(NFARES)

Pearce, A., *The Weather Guide Book,* London, 1864

Pointer, J., *A Rational Account of the Weather,* Paris, 1887

Poste, E., *The Skies and Weather Forecasts of Aratus,* London, 1880

Prince, C., *A Literal Translation of the Astronomy and Meteorology of Aratus,* London 1895

Ring, K., *Predicting The Weather By Looking at the Moon,*

Hazard, 2000

Russell, Hon.F.,*On Cirrus and Cirro-Cumulus,* Quarterly Journal of the Meteorological Society Vol,ix,No.47

Sawyer, F., *Sussex Folk-Lore and Customs Connected with the Seasons,* Lewes; *Sussex Natural History Folk-Lore and Superstitions,* Brighton,1883

Shaw, Sir N., *Manual of Meteorology,* Cambridge. Vol i, 1926, 1932

Shepherd's Kalendar, London

Silvester, N., *Note on the Behaviour of Certain Plants in Relation to the Weather,* Quarterly Journal of Royal Meteorological Society, Vol.ii. No.217

Smith, Rev.A., *On Wiltshire Weather Proverbs and Weather Fallacies,*1873

Spedding, J., *Collected Works of Francis Bacon,* 1857-72

Stalking the Wild Magazine

Steinmetz, A., *Everybody's Weather Guide,* London, 1867

Steinmetz, A., *Sunshine and Showers,* London, 1866

Steinmetz, A., *Weather-casts and Storm Prognostics,* London, 1866

Stormfax.Inc

Srachan, R., *Principles of Weather Forecasts,* London, 1868

Swainson, Rev.C., *A Handbook of Weather Folk-Lore,* London, 1873

Swainson, Rev.C., *Folk-Lore of British Birds,* London, 1885

Systema Agriculturae: Being The Mystery of Husbandry, etc, by J.W. 1681

Taylor, B., *Weather Wisdom,* Article in *Victorian Magazine,* Dec. 1891

Taylor, J., *The Complete Weather Guide, including the Shepherd of Banbury's Rules,* London, 1814

Taylor, T., *Aristotle's Meteorology,* London 1812

The Farmers Almanac

The Popular Encyclopedia (1896)

Thorndike, L., *A History of Magic and Experimental Science,*

Vols.iii and iv, History of Science Society Publications, New Series, 4, Columbia, 1934

Topliss, J., *Observations on the Weather,* London, 1849

Tributsch, H., When The Snakes Awake, MIT Press, 1982

Tusser, T., *Five Hundred Points in Good Husbandry,* 1812

Watts, A., *Instant Wind Forecasting,* Coles, 1975

Whitaker, R., *Weather,* Nature Co., 1996

Weather Book, The: Three Hundred Plain Rules For Telling the Weather, London, 1841

Willsford, T., *Nature's Secrets,* London,.1665

Wing's Ephemeris for Thirty Years, London, 1569.

Wood, J., *Theophrastus of Eresus on Winds and on Weather Signs,* London, 1894

Woollams, Eliz., *What Do the Leeches Say?* Ca., 1859

Wright, M., *A Medley of Weather Lore,* Bournemouth, 1913

ACKNOWLEDGEMENTS

This work has come from many sources, some identifiable and some not. The author wishes to apologise if material has been used that has not been sufficiently acknowledged. To be fair, sometimes letters have been written asking for permission but they have not been answered. In such cases, the names of sources have appeared anyway, and we regret any inconvenience. Many works quoted are from out-of-print books and sources have been lost, or duplicated in a number of publications such that no clear copyright exists. Much material is traditional and therefore out of copyright anyway, but effort has been made to acknowledge where it is published. Again, apologies if this has occurred: omissions or erroneous attributions have not been deliberate. Where possible, accuracy has been our aim and intention.

Ken Ring, 2002